Existential Psychology and Sport

This book offers a radical alternative to the cognitive and cognitive-behavioural approaches that have dominated sport psychology, and represents the first systematic attempt to apply existential psychological theory and phenomenological method to sport psychology.

This much-needed alternative framework for the discipline of applied sport psychology connects to many of the real and most significant challenges faced by sports performers during their careers and beyond.

Increasing numbers of professional teams and athletes look for assistance with the psychological factors of their performance and there exists a growing body of professional sport psychologists ready to provide support. Despite this, it seems at times that there remains a significant gap between the real needs of sport performers and what is delivered by traditional sport psychology. Goal setting and 'mental skills training' can help to improve some aspects of performance but can training of this sort contribute towards an athlete's personal development – towards their journey to realizing their self-potential and becoming a fulfilled human being?

Existential psychology aims to assist athletes in their personal growth so that as they develop their physical strengths through sports coaching, they also become a stronger person, and are therefore more likely to achieve their true sporting potential. *Existential Psychology and Sport* outlines an approach that can be used to add something of depth, substance and academic rigour to sport psychology in applied settings beyond the confines of mental skills training and good listening skills.

Mark Nesti is Reader in Sport Psychology at York St John College, UK.

This book is due for return on or before the last date shown below.

Existential Psychology and Sport

Theory and application

Mark Nesti

Routledge
Taylor & Francis Group

LONDON AND NEW YORK

First published 2004
by Routledge
2 Park Square, Milton Park, Abingdon, Oxon OX14 4RN

Simultaneously published in the USA and Canada
by Taylor & Francis Inc
270 Madison Ave, New York, NY 10016

Routledge is an imprint of the Taylor & Francis Group

© 2004 Mark Nesti

Typeset in Goudy by Wearset Ltd, Boldon, Tyne and Wear
Printed and bound in Great Britain by MPG Books Ltd, Bodmin

Every effort has been made to ensure that the advice and information in
this book is true and accurate at the time of going to press. However,
neither the publisher nor the authors can accept any legal responsibility
or liability for any errors or omissions that may be made. In the case of
drug administration, any medical procedure or the use of technical
equipment mentioned within this book, you are strongly advised to
consult the manufacturer's guidelines.

British Library Cataloguing in Publication Data
A catalogue record for this book is available from the British Library

Library of Congress Cataloging in Publication Data
A catalog record for this book has been requested

ISBN 0-415-28142-3

To my mother and father
For giving me life, love and
a faith to follow

Contents

Preface

This introduction was written on a visit to Copenhagen, Denmark where I was fortunate to present a workshop on existential psychology and sport at the XIth European Congress of Sport Psychology. I prepared an outline for this introduction whilst sitting in the gardens of the Royal Danish Library just around the corner from Soren Kierkegaard Square. This was apt in so many ways not least, as Kierkegaard is accepted by most to be the founder of modern existentialism. So why did I make my notes in the gardens and not in the square itself? The simple but important answer is that the square was austere, rather unattractive and uninviting in comparison to the beautiful library gardens. Was this a deliberate act by the city authorities of Copenhagen to mark out such a sombre memorial space in their otherwise wonderful city? Maybe the city planners were also keen scholars of Kierkegaard! Either way, this experience led me to reflect once again on why Kierkegaard, existential philosophy and psychology have proved to be such a bitter pill for most to swallow. Existential approaches stand accused of over emphasizing the ugly and tragic side of life. With their focus on death, freedom and responsibility, isolation and inauthenticity, it is easy to see how it has been described as an approach for the temperamentally gloomy. Indeed, despite his warm support for much of what existential psychology had to say, Maslow (1968) was much less enthusiastic about what he saw as its overtly pessimistic spirit. He was particularly critical of its failure to acknowledge the joys and positives of life, going so far as to suggest that much of this approach reflected the miserable and painful lives of its founders and none more so than Kierkegaard himself. Which brings us back to the square and the garden!

A major difficulty with existential psychology is that much of the language used in this approach sounds strange to the modern reader. For example, terms such as, 'the-world-as-lived', 'being-in-the-world', angst and inauthenticity, are difficult to explain easily and quickly. Immediately therefore, the person wishing to know more about existentialism and existential psychology becomes aware that this task will demand considerable patience and persistence.

On a more positive note, once they have begun to grasp these unfamiliar terms and strange new words, the sport psychologist (especially those with considerable experience) will encounter some much more recognizable territory. To be existential is at least, to attend to questions around meaning, freedom, choices and responsibilities. Sport psychologists often help their clients to confront these issues, particularly when experiencing new stages in their careers or when facing retirement or serious injury. Some of the other important themes in existential psychology relate to moving forward despite inevitable setbacks. This involves working hard at being all that you can be, whilst accepting that you will never actually fully achieve this. These elements are intrinsic to competitive sport and most of sport as a whole. Indeed, it is often the case that sport provides one of the best vehicles for these life experiences, and moments of growth and deep learning. Recognition of this, alongside other potential benefits to the person and the community, is one of the reasons why sport is so valued in many societies.

According to the existential perspective, the sport psychologist exists primarily to assist the sports performer to become ever more true to themselves, and to accept that personal development is often an uncomfortable experience. As a sport psychologist however, the aim is to assist the person in order to enhance their performance in sport. Improvements of course may be seen quickly, or it could be that many years will pass before they emerge more clearly. The performance increment could be in a narrow and discrete skill, or it might relate to a broad range of factors; the location and magnitude of the change and improvement is sometimes less important than the process itself. However, the existential psychology approach is fully convinced that no real and lasting growth and development in performance can occur, unless the sports performer is prepared to engage in a personal and committed struggle towards self-knowledge.

The task facing a sport psychologist guided by existential perspectives is in fact quite modest, yet difficult to pursue. Through the use of their personality and by allowing their work to be informed by the principles of existential psychology, sport psychologists are called upon to support sports performers in their journey towards authenticity and transparency of self. This never-ending task rests upon an explicit and very definite philosophical outlook, something that separates this approach from others in psychology and sport psychology. Philosophical questions apart, existential sport psychology is first and foremost a psychological approach, and it is within this discipline and not philosophy, theology or anthropology that its usefulness must be judged.

In many ways, Part I of this book represents an attempt to identify the defining characteristics of existential psychology and how these could inform sport psychology. Chapter 1 outlines some of the most important differences and points of contact between humanistic and existential psychology. The intention here is to highlight that the older approach of existential psychology contains a powerful (and some would say unpalatable) message, that is, self-actualization is not our most important need or motive. In contrast to humanistic psychology, existentialism leaves room for both freedom *and* personal responsibility in our plans and projects. The major criticism of the humanistic approach is that it tends to downplay or ignore the negative and unappealing aspects of life, and stress that the self-centred pursuit of individual goals and aspirations is the path to happiness and success. Existential psychology accuses humanistic approaches of being idealistic and unfaithful to real life. It is this major distinction between the idealism of one approach and the realism of the other that gives rise to most of the other significant differences which exist between each.

Chapter 2 builds on this by examining some of the underpinning values and assumptions behind existential psychology. Throughout this section, consideration is given to how existential psychology differs from the dominant and traditional approaches in psychology that are derived from the natural science model. Existential psychology, according to Giorgi (1970), is based on a *human science* paradigm and this means that its history, principles and ideas are radically different to most other approaches in psychology. This is discussed and focus is directed at how the main ideas can be applied within a sporting context.

The phenomenological method and the use of existential-phenomenological methodology in sport research are introduced in Chapter 3. Phenomenology is a notoriously difficult topic to discuss because amongst other things it is an approach which rests on a rejection of the dualistic subject/object split upon which most scientific investigation is based. Again, it can easily be mistaken as advocating a return to introspectionism in psychology. Its real purpose is not to investigate consciousness per se, but what our consciousness 'does' with the phenomena presented to it. Phenomenology uses the term, *intentionality* to refer to the unified relationship between what we perceive and the object itself. This approach emphasizes that what we perceive is always something interpreted; we attach meaning to something and in turn, we ourselves have meanings ascribed to us. These difficult and dense ideas surrounding phenomenology are introduced within Chapter 3 to allow the reader to reflect on the possible use of phenomenological methods in sport research.

Part I concludes with an in-depth comparative account of how anxiety has been typically studied within sport and the existential view of this pervasive phenomenon. Chapter 4 is devoted to anxiety because this emotion is undoubtedly the most important for existential psychology. This is because existential approaches understand anxiety as something that often accompanies personal growth and self-development. In addition, the experience of anxiety is strongly connected to key existential issues such as, isolation, making choices and the inevitability of death.

Part II more closely addresses issues relating to the application of existential psychology in sports practice. This is an increasingly important area of activity for many. Within Chapter 5, consideration is given to how a sport psychologist could use an existential psychology counselling approach with their clients. The focus is not on what to *do*, but on the qualities required for those wishing to operate in line with existential perspectives.

These ideas and principles are then explored within Chapter 6 in relation to working within professional sports settings. The demands placed upon the sport psychologist operating in a professional sports environment are arguably very different to other contexts. This chapter deals with some of these issues and describes how an existential approach could inform the work of a sport psychologist operating with elite professional sports teams.

Questions around ethics and sport psychology practice are becoming increasingly important as the area seeks to define its professional role and methods of working. Existential psychology has much to offer in terms of values and ethical behaviour and some of the most important issues are touched upon in Chapter 7. It should be emphasized that the debate around ethical practice, confidentiality, client rights, and practitioner duties and responsibilities is currently high on the agenda for many reasons. This chapter is intended to provide a brief account of how an existential sport psychologist would approach the important matter of ethical decision-making and values. The reader is encouraged to engage in literature from existential philosophy and psychology to get a more complete account of this crucial topic.

Finally, Chapter 8 contains a personal account of the decision to use existential psychology to provide a framework for my approach to work with sports performers. The chapter conveys that there were a number of factors that influenced this decision and that my appreciation of the value of this approach has grown over the years. The challenges facing the sport psychologist hoping to use existential ideas to inform their practice or research in sport are many. They include, little recognition (or even acceptance) for this perspective in psychology and sport psychology, a lack of literature in the area, few academic courses addressing existential psychology and the obscure and unfamiliar language associated with existential thought. On the other side however, this approach appealed because it has rejected positivism and the natural science model as a basis for studying human persons, and it claims to be truly holistic and focused on reality rather than on hypothetical constructs and theory. The most important persuasive force was that at last, here was an approach that helped me to understand why the most powerful and rewarding sessions took place where real meeting took place between me and the client. Existential psychology provided something of depth which paradoxically (apparently) connected to the lives of the sports performers I worked with. It was able to explain why communication skills and courses aimed at developing empathy were unlikely to succeed; that personal reflection, critical evaluation, extensive reading of the great books of literature, philosophy, psychology, developing a passion for life and throwing oneself into tasks, were more likely to build genuine empathy and authenticity in dealing with others.

The case studies draw on the work I have been able to do with sports performers in a variety of settings during the last 15 years. The individuals concerned have given their prior agreement to discussing part of their journeys in sport and life. To maintain anonymity and to protect confidentiality a number of significant changes have been made to the circumstances and situations described in each case. Nevertheless, each represents a truthful account of the existential encounter between a sport psychologist and individuals involved in sport.

Finally, existential psychology called me to reconsider the 'givens' of human existence – love, life, death and meaning. It is the last of these that has been most important in my work as an existential sport psychologist. For others it may be that another 'existential given' such as human isolation is key. In my work with sports performers, the search for meaning, from micro issues to the ultimate questions around life's meaning, has been the constant undercurrent. Existential psychology is an approach for those who believe that it is only by facing up to the call to find meaning in our lives that we can give ourselves without reservation to the challenges, performances and projects we encounter daily.

Acknowledgements

Writing a book is an impossible task without the help and support of a number of people. I thank them all for their critical insights, provocative comment and encouragement. In particular, the following individuals have contributed in a unique and vital way during the past three years work on this project:

My colleagues at York St John's, especially Kate Hutchings for tremendous help with proof reading and editing and Prof. Andy Smith for giving me time and space when I needed it most. Simon Hartley, Mike Forde, Nick Watson, John Gray and Malcolm Cooke for their authenticity, critical spirit and passion.

Prof. John Osbourne, University of Alberta for introducing me to existential psychology in the 1980s and Dean at Hull University, David Sewell, for my academic growth in the 1990s.

The staff at Routledge, especially Samantha Grant and Simon Whitmore for their patient support and guidance.

Finally, to my wife Sarah and our children, Catherine, Vincent and Beth for teaching me more about life, sport and psychology than all my studies or reading ever could!

Part I

Existential psychology

Principles, ideas and research
perspectives

1 Introduction

Existential and humanistic psychology

This introductory chapter aims to briefly consider how accurate Maslow and the greater part of the humanistic psychology movement was in its assessment of the negative tenor of existential psychology. Humanistic psychology is arguably the closest approach to existential psychology and therefore provides both a point of contact and equally an ideal measure of difference. In addition, despite there being relatively few empirical studies that have drawn on humanistic psychology (Ravizza, 1977), many applied sport psychologists (e.g. Rotella, 1990; Balague, 1999) have utilized this approach in their work with sports performers.

In contrast, the cognitive–behavioural approach has been dominant in applied sport psychology for at least the last 25 years. This is seen in the plethora of publications, articles, books and conference presentations that consider the efficacy of different Mental Skills Training (MST) programmes and psychological techniques. For example, at the European Congress of Sport Psychology in 2003, the vast majority of papers addressing the role of the sport psychologist in enhancing performance discussed the use of mental skills training. The focus on MST and evaluating its effectiveness continues unabated in the area of sport psychology in spite of a number of reasons why this should not be the case. These factors will be considered in greater depth later within this introduction; however, it is worth mentioning some of the more important of these at this stage.

Mental skills training

When sport psychologists began to turn their attention to applied work and started to investigate this from a more scientific and empirical perspective, it was quite logical that various forms of MST, such as imagery, concentration skills and arousal control would be scrutinized and evaluated. However, after over two decades of such work, there are questions about how much more we need to know about this area of applied practice. In simple terms, if resources are limited (as they always are) should we not be doing other things instead? It is surely time to seriously consider the myriad of other issues which are crucial to performance enhancement work with sports performers at all levels. A major area that has received little attention so far, relates to identifying the psychological theory and overall approaches that underpin practical work with sports performers beyond MST. Some practicing sport psychologists have found their own solution to this by using sports philosophy and other philosophical material to help provide the rationale for their work. Others are often quite unable to articulate a base for what they are doing alongside MST; some are honest enough to refer to it as 'just talking!' Whilst those applied sport psychologists who rely on philosophy to fill in the gaps can be admired, it is harder to accept that practitioners in an aspiring (at least) profession are unable to explain up to 80 per cent of what they do by discussing it in terms of a sufficiently deep psychological theory or group of approaches. 'I rely on good communication skills' is hardly an acceptable account when the profession is attempting to gain credibility with other bodies and to be able to offer the sports performer something they could not get anywhere else.

Another problem with the over reliance on MST in our literature and practice (albeit very few actually deliver MST and nothing more in reality) is that these techniques are often merely sticking plasters, when much more is needed. The need to consider deeper issues and move the focus away from only managing symptoms, is something which is argued in this book and is even more important now that more coaches are quite proficient in delivering MST within their sessions. In the UK and many other countries, considerable efforts have been directed at introducing coaches to the principles and practice of MST by national coach education bodies. In addition, major sport governing bodies have integrated sport psychology awareness and MST programmes into their coaching awards and increasingly, coaches operating at the higher levels are quite able to do much of the MST work which previously only the sport psychologist could provide. This has been welcomed by the sport psychology community because the sports knowledge, credibility and accessibility of the coach means that MST can be shaped to meet the individual athlete's needs more precisely and adherence to these programmes is enhanced.

A further explanation of the little recognized dominance of MST in applied sport psychology is arguably due to the educational experiences and training of many sport psychologists. It remains the case that most people working in the UK and US within the broad area of mental performance enhancement and sport psychology have had little formal educational contact with mainstream psychology. This has resulted in a narrowness of focus and a lack of awareness relating to most approaches in the discipline beyond cognitive–behavioural and trait psychology. This can easily be seen by viewing the dominance of inventory and questionnaire based research published in the major sport psychology journals. Until very recently, most of the key undergraduate texts in applied sport psychology contained little more than an account of cognitive–behavioural techniques such as goal setting, imagery, relaxation and concentration training. Fortunately, there have been some recent and notable additions to the literature in the area. It can only be hoped that the emergence of texts designed to inform students and sport psychology practitioners about Kelly's Personal Construct Theory (Butler, 1997) and Reversal Theory (Kerr, 1997) will provide a broader knowledge base, especially for those interested in applied work. In addition, a very important book by Hill (2001) outlines the psychodynamic, humanistic and neuro-linguistic programming paradigms alongside the cognitive and behavioural approaches. This text is aimed at introducing readers to less well-known approaches from the parent discipline and considers how those may be used in work with sports performers.

These new developments should assist current and future applied sport psychologists to recognize that psychology is more than MST and questionnaires. This additional knowledge may also help those who are dissatisfied with the over reliance on cognitive–behavioural and trait based approaches to avoid seeing their option as a choice between either MST or philosophy. Practitioners and researchers may find that their efforts will be more fruitful and satisfying where they consider their work by drawing on the many approaches in psychology, such as Gestalt, Humanistic, Jungian and Existential, all of which accept their historical link to philosophy. It should be recalled that psychology as a separate and distinct academic discipline is barely 150 years old. According to May (1977), psychology and psychological questions were formerly addressed within philosophy primarily, although there are clear links between physics and the natural sciences in particular and experimental and behavioural psychology. Apart from accepting that their approaches are based on a set of philosophical assumptions, the acknowledgement of the link with philosophy is important for another reason; there is an unfortunate tendency to view the less technique-focused approaches in psychology as being impractical and vague. Anything that appears to be close to philosophy or within the domain of philosophy is viewed as something at odds with the concerns of everyday life.

Philosophers such as Pieper (1989) have argued that philosophy is concerned with asking the big questions about what we are and why we exist. In contrast, psychology is more interested in *how to*, rather than *what for*, and therefore is oriented towards action and change. However, without an awareness of the philosophical position accompanying this focus on actions, we will run the risk of pursuing a goal (means) whose final outcome (ends) is undesirable. The inclusion therefore, of a much broader range of paradigms in sport psychology and especially those that are explicit about their links to philosophy, may even encourage researchers and practitioners to develop their own level of knowledge of academic philosophy. There is little doubt, that students in particular would be less reluctant to study philosophy as part of their courses if they could see that the (Human) science of psychology was unembarrassed about its links with philosophy.

Finally, there are two other important phenomena that have been overlooked in relation to the inadequacy of relying on MST. The first of these is that, as seen in the important additions to the field by the work focusing on counselling in sport (e.g. Andersen, 2000; Lavallee and Cockerill, 2002), there is an increasing interest in approaches that can accommodate broader life issues.

These may consist of relationship problems, financial matters, media difficulties or career transition. All of these factors and many others have the potential to impact on an athlete's performance and enjoyment; however, it is unlikely that a programme of MST could help here. The growth of interest in counselling in sporting contexts and a greater acceptance that there are a wide range of approaches beyond the cognitive–behavioural will hopefully add a much needed breadth and depth to applied sport psychology work.

It is this greater preparedness to utilize counselling in work with sports performers, especially at elite levels, which is helping to reveal the weakness of much of the traditional approach in sport psychology. Several studies (Greenspan and Feltz, 1989; Russel and Cox, 2000) have highlighted that elite level sports performers at least, most usually possess excellent mental skills already. In addition, those participating in competitive sport across all ages and levels are often very aware of the range of mental attributes and skills needed to succeed, although they may not have fully acquired these yet. There are two possible reasons for this development. The first relates to the increasing awareness of coaches about the importance of mental skills for their athletes. This has led to a greater willingness on the part of coaches to teach these skills to their sports performers alongside the tactical, physical and technical elements. Secondly, the growing recognition that at the highest levels it is the psychological qualities and mental strength of performers, which is the most important to success, has impacted on those lower down. The increase in books aimed at describing how to improve concentration skills, motivation and overall psychological readiness to perform, has brought the principles of applied sport psychology closer to the serious sports person, irrespective of level. For example, Gallwey's series of books on *Inner Game* (1974, 1979) and work by Orlick (2000), Loehr (1991) and Beswick (2000) have been skilfully written to appeal to sport psychologists, coaches and anyone interested in improving their mental approach to sport.

This growing exposure to sport psychology and mental training, and the increase in attention being devoted to the area by coaches, has arguably also resulted in an unforeseen and promising new development. Expressed in stark terms, the significant increase in knowledge about mental skills and their importance has not necessarily led to a greater use of these skills in practice. According to Bull and Shambrook (1998), many athletes struggle to adhere to MST programmes in the first place. Of those who do learn them, it has been reported that optimal psychological states are experienced very rarely. Ravizza (2002a) has reported that even at the very highest level of competitive sport, where athletes generally have considerable mental resilience and psychological skills, they only experience flow like states or peak experiences during 10–15 per cent of the time. The fact that improved mental skills do not necessarily lead to exceptional performances most of the time, and that serious and committed sports performers often struggle to stick to MST programmes in the first place, suggests something else may be needed.

Recently, a number of studies have suggested that sports performers are dissatisfied with the focus on MST alone and have indicated that something more is required. Research findings with elite professional cricketers (Hartley, 1999) and national level youth ice skaters (Nesti and Sewell, 1999) revealed that sports performers are searching for more than mental skills and psychological techniques to assist their efforts during training and at competitive events. It is becoming clear that much of what they are looking for relates to developing self-knowledge and having an opportunity to discuss their broader life concerns with someone other than their coach, parents or friends. Much of what takes place in meetings between sport psychologists and their clients appears more like a counselling session than a MST programme. This is now being reflected in the work of several experienced and well-respected figures in the field. In particular, the accounts provided by Andersen (2000) in relation to the initial intake session, Petipas *et al.* (1996) with student-athletes, and Lavallee and Cockerill (2002), indicate that counselling based approaches in sport are becoming increasingly recognized and valued.

Whilst the learning of mental skills may feature in a typical counselling session, this element is often much less important than within a traditional MST focused programme. Before looking at the challenges associated with this change towards the role of counselling in applied sport psychology, it is important to highlight one further factor which is especially pertinent at the higher levels of competitive sports. There seems to be an increasing awareness and a willingness to accept that personal achievement and success in sport, as in most other areas, is only encountered through and alongside moments of discomfort, pain and even suffering. What is more, there are those in the world of coaching and sports performance that criticize the prevailing approaches of sport psychology for trying to ignore this fact. As will be discussed later in this introduction and throughout the book, an acceptance that joy, elation and a sense of achievement go hand-in-hand with difficulties, defeat and failure is something which is emphasized by existential psychology. That this more balanced account of the reality of competitive sport is captured by the existential view will be contrasted with the humanistic paradigm. Humanistic psychology adopts a correspondingly positive emphasis and is coloured by a general refusal to accept that disappointments, uncomfortable moments and hardship are all inevitable and necessary elements of life.

Humanistic psychology

The humanistic model is generally accepted to have emerged in the 1960s in response to the failings of behaviourism and psychoanalysis. The major concern of humanistic psychologists and researchers was in relation to the apparent inability of the two dominant schools in psychology to address the key factors of human experience (McCleod, 1996). The type of variables they were referring to were predominantly positive and personal, such as love, creativity, responsibility, freedom and self-actualization. This represented a clarion call for psychology to redirect its attention away from the pathological and mental illness, towards a concern for the positive and healthy psychological attributes and qualities. Humanistic psychology demanded that the discipline needed to return to its very earliest roots, and following the views contained in the writings of Plato, Socrates and the sages of the East, the focus should be on an individual's potential growth and the search for personal fulfilment. Put briefly, individual human beings were seen as having the most important role in what they might become. This view is diametrically opposed to both the psychoanalytical and behaviourist positions.

Psychoanalysis following Freud, has argued that we are governed totally by efforts aimed at satisfying a number of instinctual drives and mechanisms, of which the sexual and aggressive impulses are most important. This approach conceives of human agency as something oriented towards drive reduction. We are determined by forces of a biological nature, experienced unconsciously and therefore not really within our control. Although rejecting this account as empirically unverifiable, Behaviourism shared a common underlying view of human being and personal freedom. The strictly empirical behaviourist perspective advocated by Watson (1924) and Skinner (1974), claims that we are merely the product of external environmental forces acting upon us. This paradigm argues that we are passive receivers of stimuli and our whole being and personality is shaped by these impersonal factors. For the true behaviourist, just like the orthodox disciple of psychoanalysis, there is no such thing as free will, personal responsibility and autonomy because we are totally products of either our environment or biology.

According to the major figures of humanistic psychology such as Maslow (1954) and Rogers (1961), this so-called 'third force' in psychology was based on the earlier philosophy of Humanism. This philosophical tradition, which could arguably be considered as the oldest in the West, viewed humans as the only creatures to possess free will and be aware of themselves as independent beings. Whilst not denying that biological and environmental factors are involved, this approach emphasizes that the most important influence on the formation of our personalities is in our control. The human person is assumed to have an innate quality that guides them towards what Maslow (1954) called self-actualization. This universal aspect of *human being* can never be fully satisfied and neither can it be considered as a drive or energy system. It is more accurate to say that it represents a tendency, and the response to its call is always within the individual's power and no one else.

Humanism is again at odds with the natural science foundations and deterministic basis of behaviourism and psychoanalysis due to its insistence on the uniqueness of the individual human being. This stance runs contrary to those philosophical positions such as materialism upon which traditional 'positivist' natural science is based. Through this rejection of the appropriateness of a model of science based on physics, humanistic psychology has proposed that research should utilize ideographic methods and qualitative methodologies. This of course is consistent with a belief that human persons are capable of perceiving events and acting on tasks in a way that will always be impossible to fully control or predict because of the fact of human agency or free will.

The elevation of personal autonomy and free will in humanistic psychology has received severe criticism from behaviourism, psychoanalysis and other natural science based approaches. Their major objections are that in focusing on the individual, the humanistic tradition can no longer be considered scientific, and that free will is a concept that is impossible to verify empirically. In response to these points, Giorgi (1985) has pointed out that natural science is only one type of science, and that maybe psychology would provide a more efficacious account of reality if it reconfigured itself as a human science. He has also argued that if being empirical means that, data should directly relate to reality, then the claims of psychoanalysis and behaviourism about empiricism can be challenged. After all, the psychoanalytical perspective reduces all of our thoughts and behaviours to a system of hypothetical drives, energy systems and constructs, and cannot adequately account for such singularly human traits as love, creativity and religious belief.

The humanistic psychology view of counselling tends to stress the central role to be taken by the client in any work with the therapist. Rogers' (1961) client centred approach fully captures this through its concern with the experiences and perceptions of the person within a counselling or psychotherapeutic encounter. The client is encouraged to take responsibility to discuss their future goals and choices. The psychologist is required to demonstrate empathy, a non-judgemental attitude and to attend to how the person describes their experiences and interpretations of their lives. There is a reluctance to employ intervention techniques during sessions and initial assessments of clients are usually carried out using open-ended interviews.

Rogers has carefully articulated the way in which a client-centred approach differs from a range of other traditions. There is little doubt that with its interest in developing autonomy and self-awareness in clients and taking seriously the data provided directly by the individual, humanistic psychology shares much common ground with existential approaches. Although points of a difference are relatively few, for psychologists working within an existential framework, these areas of disagreement are far from trivial or easy to ignore. This has rather forcefully been pointed out by a number of existential psychologists (e.g. Frankl, 1984; Spinelli, 1996) and it has caused much misunderstanding and misinterpretation as a result. One of the most unfortunate outcomes of this debate has been that existential psychology has been severely criticized (e.g. Maslow, 1968) and even dismissed by humanistic psychology for appearing to undermine the major tenets of philosophical humanism. For example, in contrast to an emphasis on self-actualization and the stress on the individual's choice in creating their own identity, an existential view (following Kierkegaard) would warn that freedom without responsibility is impossible (and undesirable). It has been an awkward ally for those who see the highest human goal as a project centred on the self and in contrast, has unfashionably argued that selflessness represents the ultimate aim for positive human development. In addition, those existential psychologists unprepared to ignore the harder messages of their approach have observed that the humanistic consideration of values and the growth of the person are based on the quite irrational and contradictory position, which argues that there are no permanently valid values or truths about human persons. This may sound to those outside of the humanistic and existential paradigms to be an unnecessary venture into philosophy and even metaphysics! However, this reveals as Giorgi (1985) has pointed out, that just because most other approaches in psychology are unprepared to examine their philosophical assumptions and values, it does not mean that they can avoid the fact that their work too rests on a particular philosophical perspective.

Before engaging in a more narrowly defined and systematic analysis of the differences between existential psychology and humanistic psychology, it is important to briefly consider the philosophy of Humanism. Although humanistic psychology only emerged in the 1960s, philosophical humanism can be traced back to the fifth century B.C. During this period, a group of teachers and scholars appeared in Greek society who claimed that since it was impossible to identify the truth in human affairs we could only live according to what the individual (and society) believed to represent the best choice at that time. This debate took place between the followers of Socrates and Plato, and those of the Sophists. The Platonists and Socrates argued that truth could be discovered (or more correctly, uncovered) by the human person through contemplation on reality. The term *reality* refers to the world that we experience in our ordinary daily living. It is close to the idea of phenomenology (which is the preferred research method used by existential psychology), in that attention is directed at what is immediately before us, and not at hypothetical constructs or speculative systems and theories about our lives, relationships with others and the world. The Sophists in contrast contended that since we could never approach things in a purely disembodied (i.e. objective) manner because humans are a mix of subject and object, we would never have access to the truth as such. Their solution to this apparent obstacle was to offer the young, wealthy and influential people of their time, the techniques to assist them to achieve success in the culture of the day. The less sophisticated and more philosophical of the Sophists also argued that since truth could not be acquired by contact with the external world, the only other place it could be found was within the person themselves.

This view of truth has underpinned the various strands of philosophical humanism right up to the present day. Throughout many of the various upheavals erupting across Europe this governing principle of Humanism has held sway. The common link between the Reformation, the Renaissance, the French Revolution and the rise of Marxism has been that each has, in differing degrees, attempted to locate the source of truth *within* the individual and emphasize the relativity of truth. The positive aspect of this had been that personal freedom has expanded at least in one direction, in that it has forced us to recognize more clearly that as human beings we do have a sizeable input into what we believe and how we act. However, on the down side, Fromm (1942) has suggested that whilst these historical and social movements appear to have given us a greater say in who we become as individuals and societies, this increase in freedom based on a relative view of truth and reality has left many feeling even more afraid. In his book the *Fear of Freedom*, Fromm explains how when truth and freedom exist only in so far as I conceive them, then where my freedom impinges on the freedom of another, someone following a consistent Humanist position would be unable to admonish me for this. This of course provides the philosophical underpinning to the 'unconditional positive self-regard' (Rogers, 1961) which is central to humanistic psychology counselling and psychotherapy.

In concluding this brief discussion on truth and freedom it is worth noting that Pieper has claimed that:

> Once the conviction has been lost that knowledge of the truth is what actually constitutes the mind's freedom . . . then perhaps it may come about that the concept of 'freedom' itself will grow doubtful to our understanding, vague, even obscure, we will then simply no longer know what it means.
>
> (Pieper, 1989: 107)

This profound view represents the main and some would argue insurmountable obstacle facing the Humanist thesis. In practical terms this weakness at the heart of humanism and humanistic psychology means that if the aim of life is personal self-actualization then I am entitled, indeed obliged, to pursue this in spite of the effect of this on those around me and society at large. In more brutal terms, the gap between self-actualization on the one side and self-aggrandisement and selfish egocentric behaviour on the other is too narrow to risk!

In her review of philosophical, psychological and theological accounts of freedom, Clark (1973) warned that the desire for personal freedom and autonomy cannot be the legitimate aim for individuals or society. She offers that freedom understood at the personal level cannot develop or stand alone because it always has a link to the life of the community. Further to this, she provides a critical appraisal of the humanist emphasis on our full autonomy in creating our *self*, stating that, 'to be human is to be interdependent' (Clark, 1973: 13). Again, in more blunt language and direct terms, Clark's view is that the main message of humanistic psychology could be expressed by, 'if it feels good it must be right!' This greed for personal freedom will inescapably lead an individual sooner or later into conflict with the needs and aspirations of others and the broader community. Marcel (1948), Buber (1958) and Clark (1973) have argued that it is through the idea of community and persons, rather than individuals and societies, that an authentic and constructive freedom can be built. These writers are in agreement that the all consuming focus on the self, as advocated by humanistic psychology, can never result in true community where there is a dynamic balance (and in fact a synthesis) between the projects of individuals and the requirements of societies. Clark (1973) has warned that we must reject the false idealism of humanistic psychology and philosophy. She argues that, 'Independence disguised as freedom, needs to be unmasked and recognized as spurious; it is not freedom's concretion but its contradiction' (Clark, 1973: 13).

Existential psychology

Turning away from a consideration of this foundational difference between the authentic existentialism of Kierkegaard, Marcel, Buber and others, there remains a number of important areas of disagreement. Spinelli (1996) suggests that humanistic psychology is attractive to so many because of its exclusive emphasis on freedom and choice. However, existential psychology in contrast, accuses the humanistic perspective of being incomplete, idealistic (i.e. meaning not a true reflection of reality) and liable to promote, 'a "separatist" orientation towards being which is clearly at odds with ... existential phenomenology' (Spinelli, 1996: 23–24). Existentialists refer to the idea of *co-constitutionality*, which describes the fact that we can never be known apart from the world. This interrelatedness extends to our relations with ourselves, other people and the material world. It means that it is more correct to view freedom as something which I can experience throughout my life; however, it is never encountered as a pure state. This fact is referred to as *situated freedom* by the existentialists and is an attempt to describe the reality of our existence where we know what it means to act freely within a given situation.

Roberts (1957: 8) develops this notion of situated freedom by describing the individual as being 'split down the middle – at war with himself'. He views the human as a contradictory being; someone aware that they can be free and responsible for their actions and at the same time be incapable of full knowledge about how much of their works and thoughts are influenced by constraints beyond themselves. Clearly, such a view is strongly opposed to the message conveyed (despite protestations that this is a misinterpretation!) by humanistic psychology, that we can be exactly who we want to be. Unfortunately, some existential philosophers and psychologists following the nihilistic message of Sartre, Camus and the like, have fallen into this trap of exaggerating our freedom and have confused it with licence.

Caruso (1964) has chided those relativizing trends in existential psychology which have followed this path. He suggests that those who advocate this view have merely replaced the poison of the materialist and determinist accounts of the human psyche with an antidote of such strength that it remains a poison. In denying that truth, freedom and the meaning of life can be established by science and objectively, the existentialists have made a very important contribution. However, as Caruso warns, by offering human subjectivity as the only other alternative to these questions tends to make the idea of truth, freedom and values quite meaningless and relative. Authentic existentialism has sought to avoid this unhelpful confusion by stating that reality and truth is 'out there' as it were, but that they can only be 'understood' as we experience and live them in our ordinary lives.

One of the most impressive critiques of humanistic psychology has been offered by Spinelli (1989). He is careful to point out that despite much in common, the distinctions between existential-phenomenological psychology and humanistic psychology are of considerable significance. However, Spinelli notes that most textbooks in psychology include (if at all) existential approaches within sections on humanistic and third force psychology. That this represents a general misunderstanding and more specifically a failure to examine the philosophical underpinnings and practice of each approach will hopefully become apparent in the following review.

Although not adopting an existential psychology perspective, Geller (1982: 56) was one of the first to specifically criticize the concept of self-actualization. His major concern was that the pursuit of self-actualization is, 'false, incoherent, and unworkable in practice'. According to Geller the view taken by humanistic psychology towards what constitutes the self and the reality of the human condition is fundamentally flawed. He argues that both Maslow and Rogers see the 'true self' as an inner core that is good, positive and constantly oriented towards what is right. Self-actualization refers to the situation where a person acts in accordance with their true inner self; when this is achieved the person is considered to be functioning optimally.

However, Geller raises a number of objections in relation to this. He has questioned how a person can pursue their optimal inner core, 'whose nature is essentially good and trustworthy' (Geller, 1982: 58). The dilemma as he sees it is that if the true inner self is completely good, why do I have to work hard to recognize and reconcile myself to it? Logically, something (i.e. my inner self) which tries to remain hidden from me and is difficult to access cannot be all good and trustworthy. Existential psychology has avoided this problem by stressing that the aim is not to achieve self-actualization but to become *authentic*. Authenticity as a human being refers to accepting our responsibility to make choices in our lives despite the feelings of isolation and anxiety about ultimate questions, or 'what it all means'. This is quite a different focus to humanistic psychology. In addition, the distinction between the person and their true inner self raises the spectre of dualism, where according to Geller the *self* appears to be an immaterial substance which the individual must try to discover.

Existential psychology quite clearly accepts that we are influenced by others and the world around us. It is true to say that a major focus of this approach is to clarify the client's *'being-in-the-world'*, 'by using the therapeutic context as a microcosmic indication of the client's relationship to the world' (Bretherton and Ørner, 2003: 136). This can be contrasted with the view of humanistic psychology, following Rogers in particular, for whom the core or real self is considered to be asocial in substance and origin. Indeed, this account of the self has been criticized repeatedly for sounding very close to theological and philosophical accounts of the soul and therefore obscuring the differences between the functions of psychology and psychologists on one side, and religion and clerics on the other.

In turning to Maslow's influential account of self-actualization and humanistic psychology, Geller (1982), Van Deurzen-Smith (1988) and Spinelli (1989) have claimed that it rests on a false assumption that human nature and our inner self is fundamentally only capable of good acts. For Maslow and others, destructive and evil behaviour and thoughts are never our responsibility but result (always) from the forces and frustrations caused by other people and institutions as they impinge on us. In simple terms, Maslow in particular lays the whole blame for bad behaviour on those that thwart the individual's ascent along the hierarchy of needs towards self-actualization. This means that for the humanistically oriented sport psychologist, when an athlete is 'stuck' on the hierarchy of needs where the focus is on the self-centred pursuit of fame and individual prestige (i.e. peer approval and social recognition stage), their failure to progress beyond this is always because of the indirect or direct actions of others.

Existential psychology is radically different on this point in that it rejects as 'inauthentic' the view that individuals are never to blame for their own behaviours and thoughts. This approach suggests that human beings are right to feel some measure of guilt in relation to their failings and destructive actions. However, this normal guilt must be accepted and clarified, and not pushed aside and denied awareness. According to the existential perspective, we are sometimes wholly and always partly responsible for the failings and negativity in our lives and to repeatedly ignore or suppress this fact personally will lead to neurotic feelings of guilt. Humanistic approaches tend to see evil as something that happens to us. In contrast, existential psychology contends that human beings are truly capable of both good and bad, and that we often choose each of these as much as they sometimes choose us. This relates quite closely to the existential idea of situated freedom, which states that although we do possess a real opportunity to influence what we will do and who we will become, this is constrained by our genes, environment and particular circumstances. Existential psychologists have suggested that their approach to the question of evil, the constitution of human nature, freedom and guilt, is a much more accurate presentation of real people than that provided for by humanistic psychology.

Positive psychology

Humanistic psychology adopts a positive stance and yet has been accused by some psychologists such as Calhoun and Tedeschi (1998), for leaving little room for the concept of hope within its formulations. Hope is characterized by the capacity to pursue something where success is not guaranteed. This vital element is central to existential perspectives but according to Bretherton and Ørner (2003) it is likely to be absent in a dedicated positive psychology. Humanistic psychology is most closely related to the renewed interest in positive psychology being promoted by Seligman and Csikszentmihalyi (2000). However, compared to the existential approach, the optimistic view taken by positive psychology and humanistic perspectives seems significantly incomplete.

In arguing that existential psychology is neither excessively pessimistic or optimistic, Bretherton and Ørner (2003: 137) claim that, 'Any perspective on life perpetuates a fantasy when it elevates the rich possibility of our existence without taking account of the limiting factors of the human condition (e.g. death, loss, illness).'

Some of the striking differences between humanistic and existential psychology are no doubt due to the fact that existentialism has European roots, whilst humanistic psychology 'reflects a North American attitude, which, in its emphasis on technique, can be summarized as: "If it works, do it"' (Spinelli, 1989: 159). One of the most important existential psychotherapists has observed that humanistic psychology is concerned more with peak experiences, self-fulfilment and self-awareness and less with notions such as contingency, anxiety and life's meaning (Yalom, 1980).

In attempting to examine the points of difference between existential-phenomenological psychology and humanistic psychology, Spinelli (1989) has broadened the discussion towards a consideration of the ideological basis of each approach. He has been critical of the tendency in humanistic psychology to slavishly follow the self-centred excesses of the consumer driven materialist 1970s. This interesting note has of course been challenged by others (e.g. May, 1975; Pieper, 1989). They have argued that the rapid acceptance of humanistic psychology and the human potential movement originated in the rebellious climate of the 1960s where young people in particular were enjoined to, 'find themselves' and 'drop out' of established society. Indeed, there is a real possibility that there has never been a more fertile ground for humanistic psychology than at present where at least in the West, the growth in personal wealth, philosophical materialism and global consumerism are such features of everyday life. Nevertheless, the result of all of this according to Spinelli has been catastrophic at both the personal and societal levels. In a devastating critique he claims that, 'rather than promote co-operation, humility and shared responsibility, the great majority of humanistic techniques (if unwillingly) have fostered competition, self-aggrandisement and disdain for others' subjective experiences' (Spinelli, 1989: 160).

This view echoes that of Buber (1958) who stressed that at the personal and community level, dialogue is only really possible where an individual is prepared to act on the responsibility to respond to another human being. Although Buber is referring here to the concept of *I* and *Thou* within his dialogical therapy, the inclusion of a word like responsibility in this context reveals yet another difference with humanistic psychology. Buber and most existential psychologists are in one sense claiming that all human beings are fully responsible for the lives of those they come into contact with. Such a profound and powerful idea is trying to capture the existential view that not only are we responsible for our own lives but we are faced with a level of inter-responsibility for others.

Buber describes the uninhibited and total acceptance of responsibility for another person as love. This contrasts sharply with humanistic psychology where the focus is on my responsibility to myself and loving self-acceptance replaces the existential emphasis on a selfless love for others. Spinelli (1996) has written extensively about the striking difference towards this issue between these two approaches. Again, the sticking point is centred on the differing views of what constitutes the reality of our human nature. For humanistic psychology the pinnacle is represented by the fully functioning person; this individual will have achieved self-actualization through a process of self-growth and self-fulfilment. In stark contrast, the existential position states that we are on a never ending journey, where the person is ultimately most fully themselves only when they begin to understand that the task of living involves accepting that responsibility for self and other are inextricably linked. For the existentialists, the excessively optimistic and self-making project of humanistic psychology can only be rectified through recognition that whilst we are free to become what we wish for, we remain responsible as individuals for the failings both of others and of ourselves in this enterprise. Religiously inclined existentialists such as Roberts (1957) have suggested that although it appears that the full and equal focus on the needs of others and those of ourselves is a contradiction, this is not necessarily a problem. According to Roberts (1957: 9):

> The genuinely existential thinker, on the contrary, regards contradiction as not merely the Alpha and the Omega; thought must not only begin here but must return to the given ambiguity of the human situation, and do so continually.

This critique of the humanistic tendency to equate authentic living with self-centredness has led Spinelli (1996) to emphasize that the existential perspective is always more personally demanding. He notes that most people are attracted to approaches that talk about personal growth and individual freedom. However, there is a corresponding desire to avoid any philosophy or psychology which reminds people of the difficult and even painful responsibility of recognizing that our choices and actions always impact on others as well as on ourselves. The humanistic view can lead to a situation where, 'responsibility becomes a matter for the "other" alone to deal with, and does not implicate the being whom the "other" is in relation' (Spinelli, 1996: 23–24). As Goldenberg and Isaacson (1996) have concluded, both Spinelli and Buber repeatedly emphasize that any approach which either denies our free will (e.g. Freudian), sees only free will (e.g. Humanistic) or ignores the issue of freedom and responsibility altogether (e.g. Behaviourism) will never be able to describe the reality of our human lives.

Existential benefits

Although Maslow is recognized as the founder of modern humanistic psychology, he was prepared to accept that existential psychology could offer a solution to some of the main weaknesses within his own system of thought. For example, he welcomed the existential view that rather than project our base desires and weaknesses onto the lives of others, we need to accept both our destructive and constructive tendencies are central to human nature and must be faced and integrated. Maslow chided humanistic psychology for avoiding a serious consideration of the concept of will, because of a fear that this would reintroduce associated ideas such as wilfulness, character and courage. However, for existential psychology, courage and will are important terms and not least because like spirit, character and willpower are words used by people throughout their lives and are therefore understood as signifying something real. Somewhat surprisingly, Maslow (1968) applauded existential psychology for its recognition that the most painful and unfortunate experiences in life can in themselves be of therapeutic value and that therapy is often most effective where a person comes to it during a painful episode in their lives.

In terms of counselling and therapeutic work, arguably the most important difference between the two approaches is in relation to the use of techniques. The existential position has emphasized that the central aspect of psychological work is with the *encounter* itself. An encounter involves the full and genuine meeting of the client and a therapist. According to Friedman (2002), the existential view stresses that it is when two people meet and acknowledge each other in their uniqueness and immediacy, that something worthwhile can be achieved. This worthwhile element refers to the communication taking place between two persons. It is characterized by prolonged periods where each person becomes so fully engaged in the other's utterances that their individual selves are very nearly obliterated.

Unlike with existential psychology approaches to counselling, the use of questionnaires, listening skills, mirroring, imagery, relaxation training and other physical and aural techniques is often part of the humanistic approach (McCleod, 1996). Existential psychology is considerably more reluctant to employ techniques at any stage of applied work with a client because these may serve to increase the distance between each of the parties. This is because the existential encounter is understood as providing the opportunity for a direct, and often hard hitting and committed dialogue. The introduction of techniques within such a passionate milieu must be done as a last resort. Great care is needed to avoid breaking the delicate but intensely personal thread that emerges when an encounter is happening between two persons. The risk associated with introducing techniques into 'an existential meeting of persons' relates to the problem of objectification. Briefly, this describes the corrosive power of techniques and skills that can, even despite appearances to the contrary, lead one individual (usually the psychologist) to view the other person (the client) as a case, a problem to be solved, or even a source of income and professional prestige!

Conclusion

The preceding efforts have been directed at highlighting the failings of MST in sport and at revealing the clear differences between existential and humanistic psychology. This final section outlines why an existential approach is capable of greatly adding to our understanding of sports performance at all levels and in particular for those where sport represents one of the most important factors of their lives. Existential psychology is interested in helping people to face up to the big questions and imponderables in our lives. It is relevant to all human beings because its main concerns are with issues which cross cultures, and that are independent of social class, sex, gender and historical period. The key existential questions focus on the search for meaning in our lives, our ultimate aloneness amongst our fellow human beings, and the fact of our mortality. These givens of the human condition can be repressed, suppressed or denied awareness, however, according to the existentialists, the task is to face up to these factors in spite of the uncomfortable feelings of angst or anxiety accompanying this. The aim is to become a more authentic person. This can only be achieved by continually confronting the anxiety which follows the individual throughout their lives as they courageously consider these foundational enquiries into who they are and what they stand for. Existential psychology calls upon everyone to recognize that they must make use of their freedom to search for meaning and to do this in the knowledge that there can never be a complete consummation of this task within our lives.

It is important to make clear that existential psychology can only insist that we must feed our hunger for meaning by actively participating at a personal level in the search. It cannot direct us to a particular belief system, creed or ideology. Pieper (1989) has convincingly argued that the questions surrounding which set of beliefs we subscribe to are the proper domain of philosophy and theology. He argues, especially in the modern world, just because these two sciences often appear unsure or even disinterested in arguing for a particular universal belief system, does not mean that this task is one that they can avoid. That most approaches in psychology and psychologists themselves, including (quite inappropriately) some existential psychologists, have overstepped their role and argued for a particular framework of meaning can not be excused, despite the expanding void left by much of philosophy and theology in the past 300 years. This has come about due to many very complex reasons. However, there are those such as Pieper (1989) who have explained this strange state of affairs as being also due to the degeneration of philosophy and even theology into areas more concerned with linguistic analysis, logic and systematizing rather than with questions surrounding the ultimate meaning of life.

Naturally, in such a climate it is quite tempting for psychologists to wander onto the ground largely abandoned by philosophy (and theology in some traditions). Individual psychologists who work with clients are often strongly motivated to help and despite objections to the contrary, psychoanalytic and humanistic psychology are both based on particular philosophies that see human beings as self-sufficient and capable of determining their own values. The result of this, as has been pointed out by several writers (e.g. Caruso, 1964; Assagioli, 1993) is that it is not unusual for psychologists to try and impose their own belief system onto clients either implicitly or explicitly.

Critics of the existential approach have often accused it of being more like philosophy than a branch of psychology. Existential psychologists (e.g. May, 1967) have strongly refuted this claim and in fact argue that by openly acknowledging the links which exist with existential philosophy, they are able to guard against the temptation to indulge in philosophizing. This of course is vehemently rejected most strongly by behaviourist, Freudian and cognitive psychologists who claim that as scientific approaches they are inured from any contamination from philosophy! They highlight that any approach that can accommodate notions like spiritual development (Lines, 2002), courage (May, 1975) and the transcendental (Friedman, 2002) is more a kind of philosophy or even theology, than the scientific discipline of psychology. This has been challenged by Giorgi (1970) who argues that these and other terms are important to psychologists because they affect the lives of ordinary people. In addition, he has called for psychology to be reconceived as a human science (Giorgi, 1985) in contrast to its current view of itself as a natural science based on the methods and models of physics and maths.

Unfortunately, there are even some existential psychologists who attempt to promote more than the need to search for meaning, by providing their clients with a particular meaning framework. For example, Welsh-Simpson (1998) describes how he accepts the views of existential writers and philosophers such as Sartre and Camus, in that there is no ultimate meaning and that truth is ever changing. He then proceeds to explain that a belief in the absurdity of life (Sartre) demands that we accept responsibility to create our own values and beliefs for ourselves as individuals. The main objection to this is that he has gone beyond his declared role as a psychologist following partly on existential tradition, which is to guide people in their existential search, and not to lead them to a definite set of philosophical beliefs about meaning. From a different perspective, Welsh-Simpson's post-modern outlook can also be criticized along the same lines as much of humanistic psychology. Put in blunt terms, this view merely continues the self-centred spirit at the heart of humanistic psychology which claims that my values and beliefs are all that matter. Such an approach, as Geller (1982) has pointed out, can never lead to authentic community (although a fractious society of individuals may be possible). This situation has been poignantly expressed by Sartre, the writer most associated with it in modern times, as leading to a situation where, 'hell is other people'. Clearly such a view would be unappealing in sport where teamwork, group focus and team spirit are key components in performance success.

2 Existential-phenomenological psychology
Ideas and relevance to sport

Introduction

Existential psychology has had a long and distinguished history in continental Europe, however, little was known about this approach in the USA until Rollo May introduced it in his book *The Meaning of Anxiety* which was first published in 1950. Since that time psychologists at the Department of Psychology at Duquesne University, Pittsburgh, have made a major contribution in the area by attempting to develop and articulate, in a systematic and rigorous way, psychology conceived as a human science. In over 30 years of research and scholarly output, Duquesne University has done more than any other in the English-speaking world to support an approach to psychology that draws on the insights of existential-phenomenological philosophy. The main aim has been to attempt to reconstitute psychology as the science concerned with the study of how human beings, as *persons* rather than as *things*, make sense of situations and experiences. The focus is on what something *means* to a person. To achieve this, effort is directed at the phenomena themselves as they are experienced and as they present themselves to the person. According to Giorgi (1970), this represents an even more strictly empirical way of working than exists in natural scientific psychology. However, before investigating these claims more fully it may be helpful to examine the roots of existential psychology in greater detail and consider how it differs from some of the more familiar psychological paradigms and schools.

Existential psychology has been described by Giorgi (1985) as an approach which rejects the natural science orthodoxy that has dominated psychology since its earliest days. Particularly in the field of learning theory but also in much of experimental psychology as a whole, the discipline has modelled itself on the methods of physics. Giorgi has argued that it has often been an unwitting supporter of a rationalistic, materialistic and Lockean view of the world, where the person is viewed as exclusively a product of the environment. According to Fischer (1970), the clearest examples of this can be seen in psychoanalysis and behaviourism, in that both share a common view of the human being as a determined organism for whom notions such as *freedom*, *responsibility*, *anxiety* and *courage* are meaningless terms.

Existential psychology is primarily aimed at articulating psychology in such a way that human beings can be approached and studied as persons rather than as things, drive reduction organisms, or passive receivers of stimuli. The focus is on investigating how persons participate in and bring meaning to the situations experienced in their lives. In attempting to achieve this, existential psychology is often linked to phenomenological methodology where attention is directed at the *Lebenswelt* or 'the-world-as-lived'. The aim is to return to a consideration of things themselves; that is, focus must be on the phenomena and how these are experienced and appear to the person. In other words, the approach emphasizes that the starting point for all psychological enquiry must be with the subject's pre-reflective lived experience of the event and not with some idea of how the thing ought to be experienced or perceived.

Existential-phenomenological psychology focuses on the descriptions and meanings that a person provides in relation to an experience or situation. Effort is directed at avoiding the use of labels and abstract (psychological) terms, and the psychologist is required to avoid imposing their own beliefs and perceptions about a phenomena which the subject or client is describing. This involves the use of what Husserl (1970) has called 'Bracketing'. It requires the psychologists to take steps to reflect and identify their own preconceived perceptions of the phenomena being considered. This involves taking care to hold their own views in abeyance to allow the subject or client to describe in their own words the meaning that a particular event or experience has for them. A more comprehensive account of the importance of phenomenological methods and the process of Bracketing, also referred to as phenomenological reduction, will be considered later in this section and in Chapter 3. Before leaving this issue, it is important to highlight that according to Merleau-Ponty (1962), whilst we must strive to complete the task of phenomenological reduction, complete reduction is always impossible. This recognizes that as a subject ourselves, we are not in a position to make fully explicit all that we believe about anything.

Existential psychology and phenomenology are based on a common foundational philosophy, which rejects as its starting point the Cartesian dualism that separates subject from object. Whether it has been acknowledged or not, natural science based psychology has proceeded from the philosophical position that it is both possible and desirable to look for cause and effect relationships to explain people's behaviour and thoughts, and that these can in turn be categorized, measured and analyzed. In contrast, the existential-phenomenological approach eschews any interest in searching for causes and concentrates on identifying what an experience or situation means to a person. This approach denies that it is possible for us to carry out psychological research or therapy by attending exclusively to either objective data, or subjective reports. The existential-phenomenological position however is not merely equivalent to that proposed by those advocating an interactionist approach, where reality is conceived of as a mix of both the subjective and objective.

Valle and King (1989) have suggested that a major misunderstanding has held back the acceptance of this approach into the mainstream of psychology.

Existential-phenomenological psychology is not about a return to the purely subjective introspectionism of the nineteenth century, but represents more of a middle ground between purely objective and purely subjective approaches. This can be more accurately expressed by highlighting that this approach has been described as an effort to go beyond the whole notion of the subjective/objective continuum, by emphasizing that our pre-reflective perception in one sense bursts through this artificial split because what we experience directly is the phenomenon itself. This makes it clear that such a view stresses the inseparate-ability of the subjective and the objective and therefore talk of objective, subjective or mixed subjective/objective perception is unreal and unfaithful to how human beings live in the world.

Existential psychology differs markedly from other approaches in psychology because of the methods it employs, as briefly outlined above, and because of its interest in questions surrounding our existence. These will now be considered in some detail and attention will be drawn to a consideration of the very different philosophical underpinning of this approach in comparison to other schools in psychology.

Existentialism: philosophical roots

To many psychologists, any mention of the need to investigate the links between their work and philosophy seems like a desire to return the discipline to its pre-scientific status, which they hoped it had escaped from over 150 years ago! Indeed, there are even some philosophers who would add their support to this and have warned psychology to concentrate on pursuing its science without entering into a debate for which it is often deficient in knowledge and under-standing. However, despite these protestations of purity, there are those who are prepared to confront the fact that not only the methods of psychology but also those of science itself rest on philosophical presuppositions. As Schneider and May (1995) have argued, that psychology appears unaware or uninterested in this, does not mean that it is not a fact or something of considerable importance to both the theory and practice of the discipline.

Existential philosophy emerged in opposition to the philosophical systems of Idealism on the one hand and Materialism on the other. Idealism reduces humans to their subjectivity; we are conceived of as mere thinking beings. Reality is in our minds as it were, and does not exist beyond this (and that even if it did, we can never know it as such because we always see things through our intrinsic subjectivity). Materialism in its various forms is associated with the idea that reality is made up of empirical facts that exist completely independent of mind. This position argues that the world and things in it can be known objectively and that everything that is objective is real. Existential metaphysics following St Thomas Aquinas in the thirteenth century and existential philosophy drawing on the writings of Pascal in the seventeenth and Kierkegaard in the nineteenth century challenged these views and provided a way out of ration-alism, materialism and idealism.

Existentialism according to Clark (1973) is concerned with providing an alternative to the materialist and idealist positions, and in so doing, offers a way through the old subject–object dichotomy which has bedevilled Western science and psychology since the Reformation in the sixteenth century. The high point of the materialist view and its concomitant belief in the principle of determinism is located between the period of the French Revolution and the theories of evolution, and includes the works of Freud at the beginning of the nineteenth century. This heralded the dawning of logical positivism in science, which claimed that only those things that could be measured and scientifically verified were real. Whilst Descartes much earlier, had tried to keep the determined matter of human being separate from their free minds, apart from Kant a little later, the accepted view of the scientists and most of the early scientific psychologists was that everything has a material cause and is determined. Existential philosophy, especially following Kierkegaard, rejected the view of the positivists, based as this was on materialism, objectivism and reducing everything we do to mechanical cause and effect relationships. Unlike later versions of existentialism (e.g. Sartre), he claimed that neither objectivism with its belief in only that which was publicly verifiable, or subjectivism which accepts only our thoughts and emotions as being real, could help us understand ourselves. Kierkegaard saw clearly that it was only by adopting a bifocal perspective that we could manage to see ourselves as we truly are. In simple terms, he objected to holding a view of our thoughts and actions in ways that could only satisfy the philosophers and scientists rather than our own experience of existence.

Although considered by many as the author of modern existentialism, Kierkegaard (1813–1855) was in fact continuing on a tradition, which could trace its roots back to Pascal, Aquinas and Socrates in the West and to some elements of Taoism and Buddhism in the East. These spiritual leaders and religious and philosophical ideas all considered the questions surrounding existence to be fundamental to our development as individuals and communities. Interest was directed at *being*, which really refers to how we understand what it is to live our lives in this world where nothing can ever be known or predicted with total certitude, and where we will eventually cease to exist. It is this last condition of human being which existential philosophy has had much to say about, and it may be argued that this has led some to criticize it for what seems like a morbid and excessive interest death. However, before looking more closely at this, it may be useful to draw out the key philosophical ideas normally associated with existentialism.

Existentialism according to Valle *et al.* (1989) is the name that describes a number of closely related and similar philosophies. The prime concern of existential philosophy is to seek to attain an understanding of the human condition, 'as it manifests itself in our concrete, lived situations' (Valle *et al.*, 1989: 6). Attention is directed at considering our physical dimension and also our experience of freedom, joy and suffering and our reactions to these and other elements of our lives.

Existentialists generally accept that natural science approaches based on the philosophy of logical positivism and materialism can provide useful accounts of the physical aspects of life but are incapable of saying anything worthwhile about the emotional life of the individual. The solution they advocate is to emphasize that human beings are not just objects or things in nature and that they exist in a 'total, indissoluble unity or interrelationship of the individual and his or her world' (Valle *et al.*, 1989: 7). This can be understood to mean that the person and their world are inseparable and therefore to view the person apart from the world, or indeed the world apart from the person, is an impossibility. The existentialists refer to this as *co-constitutionality*; to view the person one has to view their world simultaneously. Or put another way, any attempt to study humans as if they were pure matter or pure mind is an abstraction and as such, can never get close to the reality of how our lives and the events in them are truly lived and present themselves to us. This leads onto a further distinction which existential philosophy has called *situated freedom*. This refers to the belief that as the world is always influencing the person and the person is constantly engaged in shaping their own life, absolute free will and its opposite, total determinism is impossible. This places existential philosophy alongside the major theistic religions of the world but out of step with the dominant philosophical views over the last 300 years. Both the Judeo–Christian traditions and the earlier existentialist philosophers have consistently taught that freedom is real and that not to acknowledge this, as have philosophers such as Comte and Locke, results in abstract systems of philosophy that do not stand up to the ultimate test of providing a truthful and recognizable account of our everyday life.

Existential philosophy postulates that the best way to understand human nature is to investigate it as it presents itself to us in everyday life, rather than through the lens of particular theories. Existentialism suggests that the focus should be on understanding those things that are unique to human beings and which separate us from every other creature. For example, they argue that philosophy and psychology should direct their efforts at understanding choice, love, responsibility and an awareness of our own mortality. These and other similar experiences can only be understood in any meaningful way by going to those closest to the lived experience, that is, the individual as they find themselves in the particular situation. The aim is to access what something means to the person who has experienced the event, and crucially to achieve this without encouraging any pre-reflection or looking for a natural explanation. This relates to what May (1977) has called the *natural attitude* and is closely associated with scientism, which refers to the tendency to look for cause and effect relationships in all circumstances.

Existential philosophy is more accurately described as a range of philosophies each of which share a number of key concerns. Before looking at some of the different approaches in existential philosophy, it is important to briefly describe the elements that feature most strongly in existentialism as a whole. Existential philosophy is primarily interested in efforts directed at understanding what it means to be a human being. Whilst almost all philosophies would claim to share this focus in some way or other, the particular interest of the existentialist philosopher is aimed at discovering what it means to exist as a human being at its most basic level. In other words, they are attempting to approach and understand our lives as they are lived by each one of us directly and immediately. This has been referred to by Heidegger (1962) as involving a focus on our *being-in-the-world* and can be translated as describing how we truly are, prior to reflection on who the world thinks we are. This means that existential philosophy is concerned with understanding (it may be more accurate to say with self-understanding) and with clarifying what it means to live our lives beyond, or more correctly, prior to an awareness of our roles and functions as, sister, father, teacher, athlete, unemployed, surgeon or burglar! According to Schneider and May (1995: 53–54), 'existential philosophy attempts to clarify the life-designs or experiential perimeters within which we live. What are their shapes, existential philosophers ask, and how much freedom, meaning, value, and so on do they permit us?'

In summary, existential philosophy is directed at questions of a deep and personally significant level such as, what does it mean for us to be aware of our own mortality, is freedom fully attainable or a mere illusion, and are we responsible for our actions or is this governed by our genes, environment and fate?

Existential philosophy has concerned itself with the distinction between *existence* and *essence*. These terms relate to how much freedom we have in establishing the basics of what it is to be a human being. The debate centres on the idea that there is such a thing as human nature and human being, which is distinct from that of all other creatures, and whether this is by and large a fixed and universal phenomenon or an open-ended and continually evolving project.

Some existentialists such as Sartre, have claimed that our existence precedes our essence. For Sartre, this means that there is no human nature as such. He suggests that to talk about our essential humanness (i.e. essence) is to beg the question about how this was created in the first place, which in turn leads back to the need to find an ultimate creative source or God. However, there are many existentialists, for example Kierkegaard, Marcel and Gilson who contend that essence precedes existence. These philosophers have taken a stand by this and affirm that human nature and human being are givens, although how these exist and present themselves in the world varies across time and place. This key area of disagreement between different existential philosophers will be considered briefly in the next section. This will reveal that existential philosophy is quite clearly not a unified and homogenous body of knowledge, and that the points of disagreement have resulted in arguably two very different interpretations concerning the important existential questions around freedom and responsibility. However, there are several general characteristics that are common to existential philosophy irrespective of its views on the essence–existence debate. These will now be considered in turn before exploring the points of divergence amongst some of the key figures associated with this approach.

Existential philosophy can be conceived as a reaction against other philosophical approaches, which assume that a purely logical, rational and systematic study is the best way to proceed in order to understand issues such as truth, knowledge and the other traditional concerns of philosophy. The existentialists reject any view that regards humans as objects or things and they reject the tenets of naturalism, which sees human beings as just one other animal amongst all others in the world. Existential philosophy accepts that we have much in common with other living creatures, however it argues that a special place be reserved for humankind because we are aware that we are aware! Another way of expressing this is that the existentialist perspective argues that only the human person is fully conscious of themselves (i.e. capable of self-consciousness) and that they alone of all living things on the planet, are able to reflect on their own projects for the future, present or past.

Existentialism lays particular emphasis on the fact that we are alone in being aware that we must ultimately die and that this unavoidable condition, which faces us all as individuals, is the most important point of our existence. According to the existential philosophers, that people at certain points in history and within their personal lives try to forget about or ignore this fact, does not diminish its centrality in understanding the human experience and ourselves. Indeed the existentialists are united in portraying the failure of people and societies to face up to the questions associated with an awareness of our mortality as deeply worrying and a sign of a profound imbalance in our mental outlook.

In relation to this, most existential philosophers stress that philosophy should remain open to a consideration of the spirit and the transcendental dimension in human existence. They are not claiming that philosophy must move into the area where the great spiritual and religious traditions operate, and neither do they feel it appropriate to engage in debates normally within the preserve of theology. However, they are highlighting in their view, any philosophy worthy of the name should have something to say on those aspects that are most unique to humankind. That this includes a consideration of topics that other philosophies often ignore makes their task even more necessary. For example, questions around love, freedom, whether there is meaning in our lives or meaninglessness, the necessity of choice and the degree of responsibility for our actions represent the main areas of interest. That each of these according to existential philosophy, provides a great challenge in terms of understanding because of their fundamentally ambiguous nature does not lessen the need to try to grasp their meaning for our lives.

Most views in existential philosophy accept in some measure that a full understanding of these and other important existentially significant issues can never be attained given that we are never able to detach ourselves completely from a consideration of things in themselves. This *embodied freedom* involves an acceptance that we are neither fully free nor completely determined, but as Merleau-Ponty (1962: 518) says, we are an 'inextricable intermixture'. Given this reality of human being, it is clear why existential philosophy holds that we must remain open to a sense of mystery as we pursue knowledge about these foundational elements of human existence. The exhortation emanating from the existentialist philosopher is that we must refrain from looking for the simple explanation, which a closer examination often reveals, is actually an explaining away. They also warn that we must not be tempted to follow the opposite path, involving as it does a refusal to consider the more important aspects of our existence because full knowledge about them is unattainable. This position of course is anathema to those like Wittgenstein and the materialist philosophers, who advocated that we should only consider those things that we can say something definite about; the rest should be left well alone!

Existentialism can be conceived of as an approach that denies that truth is best discovered by following a rational, systematic, logical and purely intellectual path. This is more sharply expressed by pointing out that it is often the case that truth, whether scientific, moral or of any other kind, can only really be understood where it is grasped personally, rather than only understood or known about in a more impersonal and theoretical way. Existential philosophy accepts that common sense and science can reveal a fact or a truth *about* something; however, an understanding of broader and deeper matters cannot be acquired without our full participation in the situation or issue. This has been summed up in the statement which claims not everything that is objective is real. In other words, there are two categories of facts; those that can be approached without our involvement and those that can only be fully understood where we take a stand in relation to them.

Existentialism and psychology

Related to this is that existentialism as a philosophy, and from a psychological perspective, describes the human situation as being essentially ambiguous. This refers to the existential fact that human beings are always engaged in a struggle between freedom and feelings of powerlessness. They are able to experience deep despair one moment and the most intense and profound joy in the next. They are aware that they are individuals and that some day they will die, but they are also part of a community of fellow human beings and because of this, can give and receive love. All of this places us in the situation of never being able to know for certain what to do with our freedom and being unable to avoid the need to confront this uniquely human challenge, although we all try to escape from this throughout our lives in various ways. This apparently paradoxical position has been captured by Roberts (1957), in pointing out that everything would be straightforward if we were merely animals or God! As animals or God, we would be free from consideration of what to do with our freedom and be freed from the mental anguish that comes from making moral choices. However, 'so long as we remain human we must enter into the mystery of what it means to be a finite self possessing freedom' (Roberts, 1957: 9).

According to existential philosophy and psychology, the main task facing each of us is to live an *authentic life*. Authenticity may never be fully achieved but involves accepting the need to make choices and decisions despite the anxiety which inevitably accompanies this, given that we can never be sure of the outcome. Continually ignoring this call towards authenticity will result in *ontological guilt.* This describes the frustrations, feelings of regret and ultimately the deep despair, which we experience as a direct consequence of abdicating our responsibility to accept our freedom and choose a particular course of action. One of the ways people attempt to ignore the call to live authentic lives, is to conform to the views of public opinion, or to accept what is the prevailing orthodoxy in any area of life without having thought about this for themselves. According to the existentialists, this course of action is bought at a great cost. Kierkegaard has expressed this most powerfully by claiming that this lack of courage to think and act authentically results in the loss of the most important part of ourselves, which he calls *the self*. Without the recovery of this self or psychological core, we are unable to face up to the need to grow as a person and are liable to be even less prepared to confront and move through the normal anxiety which we encounter in our lives daily.

In addition to this focus on freedom and responsibility, all of the different philosophical traditions within existentialism stress that we must recognize a number of ontological characteristics that all humans share. This list includes the ideas of intentionality, the daimonic, freedom, destiny, anxiety and courage. Each form the core of our existence as human beings and our goal in life is to find a way to integrate these into our personalities and the fabric of our daily lives. Arguably, the daimonic, which describes our tendency to do evil and engage in destructive tasks, represents the most controversial element, at least for those followers of various humanistic philosophies and Humanism itself. This has been defined as any aspect of our human nature that has the potential to consume our whole being and lead us to pursue this despite the pain and suffering caused to others along the way. Intentionality describes the human involvement in knowing and perceiving. This refers to the fact that what we intend to do with something contributes to its meaning for others and us. For example, fire can be something to give light or to burn garden rubbish; in this sense we participate in giving some meaning to an object or event. Destiny describes the experience of being faced with choices and actively choosing. In addition, the existentialists emphasize that whilst fate involves a handing over of personal responsibility to forces beyond the self, destiny in contrast is grasped by the individual who accepts that they have some responsibility in what is happening to them. Their task is to move forward despite being uncertain of the eventual outcome and to remain self-conscious about what is taking place as they confront each situation.

Existential philosophers have claimed that the goal for each person to aim towards is an integration of these six elements and that a psychology drawing on existentialism should work towards this outcome. Before turning to how existential psychology goes about this task, it is important to note that existential philosophers and psychologists can be divided into two distinct camps, each having something very different to say about freedom, authenticity and human nature itself. One group contains some of the earliest to be associated with existential ideas such as Pascal, Kierkegaard, Buber, Tillich and Marcel. For these individuals the stress upon the importance of freedom, responsibility, the need to search for meaning in life and the fact of our mortality, all lead to the idea that there is an ultimate purpose to our existence. For them this comes down in turn to a belief in a source of all existence, namely God. According to Roberts (1957), the other group is made up of Sartre, Camus, Jaspers and Heidegger and they are united in their competing explanation of freedom and meaning. For them, true freedom and authentic behaviour is only possible when we accept that there is no given or ultimate meaning to life and that our task is to face up to this. Following from such a position, it is easy to see how these philosophers claim that there is no such entity as human nature and that all values, ethical systems and beliefs are completely relative. Such a view argues that since we are totally free to choose who we want to be, the major task of our lives is to face up to this freedom and to make choices and accept that ultimately, in the words of Sartre, we are nothing more than, a useless passion! This position is associated with post-modernism; this being the view that since there are no fixed or permanent values in the world the only certainty is uncertainty itself. This brand of existential thought is most prevalent today appealing as it does to people because of its alluring message that the individual can be anything they wish to be, as long as it is their wish and not the slavish following of someone else. It has been criticized by those such as Roberts who point out that in pursuing my freedom I will inevitably impinge on the freedoms enjoyed by others. In other words, this can lead to the most self-centred and selfish approach to living.

In contrast to an awareness of freedom which can lead to a feeling of self-sufficiency, there is a recognition that our freedom can never be total and that our lives are a mixture of happiness and joy and sadness and despair. Not to accept this reality in relation to our existence can, according to Pascal and the others, lead to a kind of stoic self-assertion and an inflation of the concept of personal freedom. This can logically proceed to the rather unhappy position where ideas of self-giving, self-sacrifice and even love are impossible. Interestingly it is this side of existentialism which has been most popular during the past 40 years. This is quite easy to understand given that it contains a very attractive message for our more individualistic age, and some have claimed that it provided a needed challenge to the more rigid and constrained freedom of former times. However, Caruso (1964) has warned that such an antidote to the narrow determinism, rampant in much of science and philosophy during the first decades of the nineteenth century can become a kind of poison if excessively used. He argues that authenticity and freedom are only worthwhile and true when they are located alongside an interest in community and the common good. In other words, freedom must be always accompanied by responsibility to avoid being the totalitarian pursuit of my fulfilment at any cost.

Existential psychology: key concepts

According to Giorgi (1985), existential psychology is primarily interested in questions which seek to address themselves to what something means to a person, rather than an analysis of why something occurred in the first place. He has claimed that this approach is consistent with psychology conceived as a Human science. This places existential psychology at odds with all other major accounts of what are the legitimate methods and subject areas for study in psychology. Focus is directed at understanding human events and experiences through an analysis of the descriptions provided by the people who are living these moments. This usually involves the use of interviews, completion of reports or diaries, or other similar qualitative research techniques. The aim is to allow the individual to convey what something means to them in the richest detail and most personal way possible. According to Schneider and May (1995), existential psychology resists the use of questionnaires and other similar data-generating techniques because these tend to interfere with accessing the material in the most direct way. This is because existential-phenomenological psychology is interested in the 'world of everyday experience as expressed in everyday language; that is the world as given in direct and immediate experience' (Valle *et al.*, 1989: 9). Again, this is why in therapeutic encounters or during research activity, every effort is made to get the client or subject to describe their experiences in everyday language rather than the conceptual terms and theoretical labels of the scientific psychologist. This relates to a further important element variously called the *Lebenswelt* (i.e. the-world-as-lived) or the life-world. These terms capture the important idea that, 'the life-world is prior to reflective thought' (Valle *et al.*, 1989: 9); it refers to our thoughts about something before we have moved on to direct our mind to a search for an explanation of something. It is similar to the difference between being captured emotionally by a beautiful piece of art, and seeking a technical and intellectual account of what makes it so.

According to Cohn (1997), there are those who define existential psychology in terms of what it is not, rather than what it actually is in theory and practice. This is understandable given that in many ways it is an approach that emerged in response to a perceived failure by other schools of psychology to see the person in their real world, where they alone exist and make their way through life. During the early part of the twentieth century, a small but prominent group of psychologists from both Freudian and Jungian traditions became increasingly interested in the problem of freedom and human nature itself. In particular, they were dissatisfied with the over reliance on traditional scientific methods which, they viewed, paradoxically, made some of their work much less empirical than was claimed. They also felt that their work was often driven by theories which did not always stand up to scrutiny when compared to the real world experiences of their patients. In addition, as Schneider and May (1995) have argued, these psychologists were reluctant to follow the prevailing mood of American and British psychology, which was preoccupied with the application of technique and a focus on addressing symptoms and not the underlying causes. Related to this, May has pointed out that for much of the past 100 years, 'we have tended to overlook the fact that technique emphasized by itself in the long run defeats even technique' (Schneider and May, 1995: 88).

One of the most impressive accounts of existential psychology has been provided by Maslow (1968). He claimed that existential psychology contained major areas of agreement with humanistic psychology but that it also contributed much in addition, especially in terms of highlighting the need for psychology to recognize its philosophical underpinnings, and to consider both the destructive and positive sides to human nature. According to Maslow, a major contribution from existential psychology is that it emphasizes that the goal of therapy should be to work towards the integration of who we are and what we have the potential to become. This means that we need to recognize that psychological health does not reside in either a repression of our more spontaneous and lower level needs and neither can it be attained by allowing a free reign to these desires. In addition, existential psychology claims this also will bring a realization that given these competing aims in our nature, 'some problems must remain eternally insoluble' (Maslow, 1968: 11).

Another important and radically different facet of existential psychology is that it stresses that we possess freedom and an inescapable responsibility to form our own personality. This view contends that we ourselves, and not our early experiences, heredity or social environment have the key role in influencing who and what we will become. In order to face up to this existential fact, and to act on it, we need to develop strength of *will* and *courage*. These terms may sound rather old fashioned and unscientific; yet according to the existentialists, they are worthy of our attention because they are meaningfully experienced in our everyday individual lives.

Maslow has also pointed out that the existentialists' claims about the uniqueness of the individual has major implications for research and practice in psychology. Specifically he suggests that single subject designs and the idiographic approach need to become more acceptable in psychological investigation. He adds that in agreement with Giorgi (1970), 'If the uniqueness of the individual does not fit into what we know of science, then so much the worse for that conception of science. It, too, will have to endure re-creation' (Maslow, 1968: 13). Following from this emphasis on the uniqueness of the person, it is easy to understand why existential psychology should insist that the only way to gain an adequate understanding of someone is to enter into the individual's world, to see it as they see it. This type of empathy is more than a skill or technique according to the existentialists and demands that whether in the research setting or therapy, the psychologist is required to lose themselves in the other in a moment of total self-giving. This has been referred to by Buber (1958) as the *I–Thou* encounter. When we meet the other person in an *I–Thou* relationship we forget ourselves and communicate with them in an intense and exclusive mode. This could be described as being in a conversation where we are in a deep flow state (Csikszentmihalyi, 1975). Buber has differentiated this type of encounter, where genuine empathy is possible, from our more usual mode of communication, which he calls, I–it. Whilst in this way of relating, we cannot achieve any real sense of empathy with another individual because we have not approached them as a person but as a 'thing', that is as a patient, client, subject, or as a problem or a solution. In other words, they are not really present to us as themselves, but are what they mean to us *beyond* themselves.

Finally, Maslow has pointed out that existential literature encourages psychologists to accept that abstract, analytical and scientific concepts and terms cannot capture everything that is meaningful to us in our world. For example, there are clearly areas of human experience such as love or feelings of forgiveness that can arguably be described better in other than scientific language. There are also other areas of life, especially those involving great joy or tragedy, where a more truthful account is likely only if we return to a consideration of the primal experience itself prior to any conceptual categorizing or technical labelling.

May (1977) has provided one of the most succinct and clear accounts of existential psychology. He has identified that the most important question facing psychology is to aid people to face up to the need to find meaning in their lives. As psychology rather than philosophy or theology, the focus is not on identifying one particular framework of meaning or another but to assist the person to accept that the *search* for meaning is a legitimate task and represents an essential part of life. Anxiety is considered to be a universal human experience; according to May its core is always anxiety about existence. This is considered to be something quite natural and indeed an unavoidable aspect of being the only creature who is aware that they exist and yet they will eventually die. This *existential anxiety* has the potential to be either constructive or destructive, and our response to it will determine whether we will grow as persons or retreat and suffer from a diminution of our *selves*. Anxiety has been identified by existential psychology as the most important human experience. Given its importance and centrality in this approach it will be considered in-depth within Chapter 4, however, it is important to clarify that it is inextricably connected to almost all of the key terms used in existential psychology and therefore some discussion of this is now necessary.

Existential anxiety

Existential psychology views anxiety as an experience that all human beings encounter throughout their lives. According to May (1977) and Kierkegaard (1844/1944), anxiety occurs because of our human freedom; freedom really means the freedom to choose one option or another in the knowledge that we can never be fully certain of what the outcome will be. The most universal and basic root of anxiety relates to the knowledge that we all must eventually die. This anxiety about existence itself permeates our individual lives according to the existential psychologists and is inescapable. However, anxiety is in a sense neutral, in that it is how we react to it rather than how it is experienced as an emotion which determines whether the impact is positive or negative.

In addressing the potential for anxiety to be beneficial or destructive, May (1977) distinguished between normal and neurotic anxiety. Normal anxiety is related to our desire to develop, grow and expand our self-awareness, and as such, is considered healthy and not something to be removed by psychotherapy or psychological techniques. The rationale for this is that learning and personal growth invariably involve the moving away from previously held goals or knowledge to something new. This path from the security of an existing understanding to the fresh challenge of the new brings anxiety to the person because they are required to give up something which is really a part of who they are. This has been expressed by Hergenhahn (1999: 346) that, 'to grow as an individual, one must constantly challenge one's structure of meaning, which is the core of one's existence, and this necessarily causes anxiety'.

Although existential psychology points out that this type of anxiety is normal, it can be a problem where the individual repeatedly tries to avoid it. This can be done by refusing to accept personal responsibility for growth and by retrenching or using other ways to deny awareness of the choices that must be faced. This has been referred to by May (1977) as neurotic anxiety and really amounts to the anxiety experienced as a result of repeated failure to face up to the discomfort of normal anxiety.

This whole view of anxiety is radically different to that held in most other approaches in psychology by stressing that anxiety can be understood as a beneficial experience. In addition, the existential position is unusual in claiming that although it is always an uncomfortable emotion, normal anxiety should in fact be welcomed as a sign that authentic learning and growth are taking place.

Other important aspects of existential psychology are those relating to the ideas of authenticity, death, freedom, isolation and meaninglessness. These existential concerns are faced by all human beings and are associated with the experience of normal anxiety or neurotic anxiety. The most controversial of these is arguably the existentialists' approach to death. Some (e.g. Schneider and May, 1995; Nesti, 2002) have pointed out that death may also be interpreted in a more symbolic way, for example, to refer to the feelings which often accompany retirement from paid employment or when confronted with a significant change in a personal relationship. Nevertheless, the awareness that we will all die sometime, and that this represents in one sense the opposite of all of our daily projects and strivings, inevitably brings anxiety. However, this knowledge about our own mortality can be constructive where we use this to discover values and meaning which allow us to feel committed to something, despite knowing that ultimately we will not be around to see its conclusion.

The question of values seems to be more related to the concerns of theologians and philosophers, and is not something that other approaches in psychology would consider as a legitimate topic for discussion. Existential psychology highlights that values are an important area for the psychologist to consider because all persons have a particular value system and this influences the meaning that they ascribe to experiences and events in their lives. In terms of dealing with anxiety, May (1977) has argued that the more mature and personally integrated an individual's values are, the greater their capacity to meet the threat posed by a new situation or experience. Mature values according to May, are oriented towards the common good, the future, and they embrace the notion of human freedom. A key task for the existential psychologist is there-fore to assist the person to recognize that the search for mature values will allow them to commit themselves to projects in the future, and to develop into a more healthy and integrated human being.

The notion of freedom is very important in existential psychology; the indi-vidual is understood as someone who can make a choice in relation to a situ-ation. This act of choosing is identified as more important than our genes, environment or early experiences in terms of influencing who and what we become. The task of the existential psychologist therefore, is to study what con-ditions assist the person to grow in this awareness of their freedom and to work with them as they wrestle with the anxiety that always accompanies the arena of decision and choice. Closely related to this is the idea of authenticity. The choices an individual makes and the values that they pursue must be the result of their own reflection and an acceptance of their freedom in this. In other words, living an authentic life involves the person in a risky and often uncom-fortable process where they take responsibility to find meaning for themselves rather than taking on, uncritically, the meaning provided by external sources. This could mean that values and meaning frameworks may in fact be identical to those held by external bodies such as scientific groupings, institutional reli-gions and political organizations, or they might be more individually based. To be authentic these configurations of meaning must be won personally and involve the total commitment of the self. The existentialists are not suggesting that this situation can ever be fully achieved but it is something that we should recognize, accept and work towards in our lives.

In conclusion, the implications of these ideas for applied sport psychology and counselling in sporting contexts will be considered in detail within Chap-ters 5 and 6. However, it is worth highlighting briefly here that the task of the existential psychologist is very different to that facing other psychologists. The existential psychologist must strive to see a situation or event from the side of their client. They must practice inclusion but take care not to find a particular set of answers to the problem; the role involves standing shoulder to shoulder with the client and encouraging them to confront the anxiety and/or guilt asso-ciated with a failure to accept their responsibility to choose authentically. The aim is to help the person to more clearly understand that they are not solely a product of their genes or the environment and that they can only become more fully human and move closer to fulfilling their potential where they are pre-pared to act upon the freedom which they possess as a consequence of human *being*. The continued avoidance of this may lead to neurotic anxiety, which has the effect of shrinking the awareness of the person in relation to the amount of freedom they have to make choices and accept some responsibility for these. Working with the client in this situation is more likely to be done by the clini-cal psychologist. The sport psychologist or counsellor without clinical training and knowledge is more qualified to provide an encounter for an athlete who is experiencing normal anxiety and normal guilt. In this situation, the psycholo-gist should be helping the client to wrestle with and begin to clarify what their experiences convey in terms of the key existential givens of choice, responsibility, authenticity and the search for meaning.

Existential psychology and the sports performer

Case study

A major difference between existential psychology and other approaches is that considerable emphasis is directed at encouraging the athlete to reflect on broader concerns and personally significant life issues. These may include past or current events in the athlete's life or be more related to the future. The sport psychologist's role is to assist the client to confront the anxiety associated with the consideration of important existential issues and to guide them in their attempt at making sense of these. This process of clarification is necessary according to existential psychology, in that it is through this often difficult and at times uncomfortable experience, that the client can be helped to face up to and begin to make sense of an important issue affecting their self as a whole.

The athlete had been working with the sport psychologist for over two years. After a regular period of formal meetings during the first two months of their work together, both parties agreed to maintain contact through email, phone calls and letters. In addition, meetings between the sport psychologist and the athlete continued albeit that these were less frequent and more impromptu. After a very successful early career in elite level sport, the athlete had experienced a more difficult time in terms of performance success. The work with the sport psychologist initially focused on refining existing mental skills, trying out new psychological techniques largely based on mental imagery, and increasing self-awareness and self-knowledge. Increasingly, the emphasis during meetings, and across the other modes of communication, was on the need to develop a greater level of self-understanding. This focus in turn forced the athlete to look deeper and more fully into the issues which she had left largely unexplored across the years, even though she considered these to be hugely important and strongly related both to an understanding of herself and to sports performance. The athlete expressed the need to search for values and belief systems which would help her to continue to grow in her personal life and to experience again the success that she had enjoyed during her earlier competitive career. This involved the sport psychologist and the athlete in a series of encounters and other types of contact, where effort was directed at searching for a personally and existentially significant meaning system. During these encounters, the sport psychologist worked with and alongside the client to help her to wrestle with the challenges and difficulties which are always experienced by a person searching for meaning in a world where the feeling of meaninglessness and the concomitant mood of despair is ever present in our lives.

In terms of how this process is facilitated and supported by the sport psychologist, it is important to highlight that their function is to accompany the client along the journey. This means that sometimes the sport psychologist will guide and take the lead in the process and at other times, the athlete will assume more responsibility for the direction of the encounter. This can only be achieved where the psychologist maintains a deep empathy for the client throughout the session and in particular at those junctures when the material being discussed is difficult to understand or deal with emotionally. For example, the athlete in this case devoted much time to reflect on a serious illness faced by an important mentor in her life. This led to an attempt to understand this tragic situation more fully and to reflect on how one can begin to make sense of both the good moments, and crucially, the inevitable, sad and less welcome aspects of life. Such a project cannot be undertaken lightly by a person, involving as it must, considerable emotional investment and repeated courage to try to find meaning in something, which in a sense, resists meaning at least in terms of a rational interpretation. The sport psychologist noted how the athlete continued to move through this process in a cyclical manner. This typically involved an attempt by the athlete to approach the issue of her mentor's illness and try to clarify why she needed to understand this for herself in a personal way. This then led onto a broader discussion centring on the need for the athlete to 'see what it all means in some bigger way', so that she could be able to deal more constructively with the setbacks experienced throughout her own sporting career and life in general, by placing these into some framework of meaning. Not infrequently, the process would go into a kind of reversal, where the athlete would struggle or even avoid following through with her line of thinking in relation to the search for meaning, and veer off course in an attempt to avoid the normal feelings of anxiety associated with this task. It is at these moments that the sport psychologist through their presence and authentic (i.e. open and honest) communication with the athlete can help keep the process alive and moving forward. This may involve the sport psychologist taking a temporary lead in the encounter, by redirecting the athlete's thoughts and reflections back to the central concern of trying to bring meaning to an unwelcome and painful event. In this case, this was helped by revisiting other difficult and challenging moments in the athlete's sport career and broader life. This allowed the athlete to reflect on the way in which she had been able to integrate both positive and negative experiences into her understanding of her career history. The athlete with the guidance of the psychologist began to recognize that without really being aware of it, she had been engaged over several years in this task of searching for a way to understand all of the many high and low points of her career. This provided the sessions with new material to consider and helped the spiral of reflection to proceed forward to return to a renewed consideration of the central concern (i.e. the need to locate the illness of a mentor into a personally chosen framework of meaning). The most important role for the sport psychologist was not to suggest possible explanations of this and other similar experiences in the athlete's life, but to confirm for the athlete that the search for meaning is an important and worthwhile task. It is of vital importance that the athlete is made aware that this is not something that the psychologist can take over in order to provide an answer to the question of 'what it all means'. The psychologist must resist the temptation to foster their own view of any ultimate system of meaning on the client, as this is beyond their boundary of operation. Their function is to support the client's increasing readiness to confront the need to search for a personally meaningful account of this situation, and to help the athlete recognize that not to accept this challenge can adversely impact on their growth as a person and can negatively affect their sports performance.

3   Phenomenology
Methodology and methods

Introduction

Although most often described as a specific method, phenomenology is more accurately a way of looking at reality. Although it has developed into a particular approach referred to as the phenomenological method, philosophers such as Kant were thought to be the originators of the idea that we could only know the world through how things appear to us. In other words, we cannot be sure of the real essence which lies behind the appearance of a particular thing. This must not be interpreted as a call to locate knowledge in our subjective perceptions. As will be discussed in this chapter, phenomenology has been credited with joining subjectivism and objectivism into a unified view of reality. According to one of its most important scholars:

> It is a transcendental philosophy which places in abeyance the assertions arising out of the natural attitude, the better to understand them; but it is also a philosophy for which the world is always 'already there' before reflection begins ... its efforts are concentrated upon re-achieving a direct and primitive contact with the world.
>
> (Merleau-Ponty, 1962: VII)

Clearly then, phenomenology is concerned with articulating our experience of the world. The way in which this is achieved within existential psychology is through adopting a phenomenological perspective on reality. The difference between this and the so-called natural attitude, which dominates most other approaches in psychology, will be considered in this chapter. Emerging from the phenomenological attitude, are several important factors that govern the use of this approach within psychological research. Although it is possible to use phenomenological method within a number of different paradigms in psychology, its philosophical orientation and practice mean that existential psychology is the approach most likely to benefit from its demands. The value of adopting a phenomenological interpretation within existential psychology and research practice will be discussed. This analysis will be extended towards a consideration of how the phenomenological method could be fruitfully employed in sports research. Despite a growing acceptance of qualitative methods within sport psychology, few studies have drawn upon phenomenology or phenomenological methods in data-generation and interpretation. However, the important work of Dale (1996, 2000) will be considered in some detail in this chapter, as these studies represent some of the best attempts at applying phenomenology in sports research.

Finally, the insights that phenomenology could provide will be explored in relation to applied work in sport psychology. This will hopefully demonstrate that the phenomenological method, especially the process of *bracketing*, its approach to questions around the idea of 'reality' and the issue of *intentionality*, are very helpful for those counselling sports performers in applied contexts.

The philosophy of phenomenology

Phenomenology owes much of its foundations to the work of the German philosopher, Husserl (1859–1938). In an attempt to devise a strictly empirical approach that could be of use to all sciences, Husserl developed phenomenology as a perspective where the sole focus would be on a person's experience of an object. According to Polkinghorne (1989: 41), this experience is not something passively received by a person but 'involves the operation of active processes that encompass and constitute the various contents that become present to awareness. These contents include not only the objects of perception but also those of memory, imagination, and feeling'. In other words, this view rejects the natural attitude of science, which is based on the idea that we can describe objects 'accurately' without having first accepted that they are literally infused with our experience of them in the first place. For example, a table is not merely a flat plane of wood resting on four supports. Instead, it is only immediately recognized by us as a table because of a meaning attached to it 'given' by our experience. The idea is that all objects are a synthesis of their objective foundation (e.g. wood surface and four supports) and the meaning we bestow on them (e.g. a table). This can be better understood if we imagine an alien arriving from another world without knowledge of the concept of a table and being confronted by such an object! That this seems to be such an obvious point does not mean that it is something which most people are aware of, or reflect on. In our day-to-day living this may not matter much. However, within the work of scientists, it could result in some very real problems, especially where the object of study is itself capable of giving other things meaning. It is because of this that phenomenologists challenge the uncritical acceptance of the natural science paradigm in those sciences where the focus of study is with thinking beings, as in psychology, rather than where interest is with non-sentient matter as in physics. This issue has been highlighted by Giorgi (1970) in his critique of psychology as a whole. He has argued that the approaches taken and methods used in psychology are mostly based on the canons of natural science. According to Giorgi, this could be remedied by reconfiguring psychology as a human science.

Some views (e.g. Sartre) propose that we can never know reality apart from our experience of it (and hence, the meaning we give to it). This sense experience is what constitutes truth as such. This position contends that there is no such thing as this or that object in the world, which is prior to our know-ledge of it. This represents the most extreme 'psychological' account of phenomenology, in that it gives total and complete pre-eminence to our sense experience. Phenomenologists following the work of Marcel (1948), Van Kaam (1969) and St Thomas Aquinas in the thirteenth century, accept that some things can only be known through the subject's experience of them. However, in contrast to Sartre and others, they 'go on to emphasize that this kind of knowledge of reality is not the only kind of knowledge of what is' (Kingston, 1961: 91). They argue that perception often involves more than what can be recorded or received by our senses. This approach to phenomenology empha-sizes that when we perceive something or experience it, our sense data and our active participation in what this data means are what we finally see and under-stand. This view of phenomenology refuses to accept the Cartesian split upon which Sartre (1958) and Heidegger's (1962) approach to phenomenology is based. This position presents reality as being both coloured by our view of it and based on something that precedes our particular take on a thing. According to some writers in the area (Roberts, 1957; Kingston, 1961), the view articulated by Marcel and others, has the added appeal because of its relation to a common sense understanding of our world. In straightforward terms, most people act as though things possess an intrinsic meaning in themselves, but accept that our experience and knowledge about an object influences how we perceive it. It seems only Sartrean phenomenologists and some phenomenological psycholo-gists such as Spinelli (1989), are unable to accept what the ordinary person already knows through their daily living and normal engagement in the world around them!

Although this issue is more related to philosophy than psychology, it is important since it highlights the differences between the two main approaches in phenomenology. The Husserlian tradition in phenomenology is prepared to bypass the question of whether the world exists as something prior to our expe-riencing it. According to Kingston (1961), Husserl did accept that the world is real; however, he advocated that phenomenology should not concern itself with this, *in order* that attention could be directed solely at our experiences. This had been considered even earlier by St Thomas Aquinas in the thirteenth century. Following this view, reality was said to exist objectively and that we know this because of our encounter with it. In other words, things in the world are intrinsically meaningful, and we can only know this after the fact of our encounter with them through a process of recollection and reflection.

Psychological research drawing on phenomenology is clearly based on an underpinning philosophy. This approach can be considered as descriptive and qualitative. According to Polkinghorne (1989), phenomenological research differs from other types of qualitative work because of its concern with the person's experience of a specific thing or event. Interest is directed at trying to capture what a particular experience means to an individual, rather than as in other qualitative approaches, where the focus is on the descriptive account provided by people *about* their behaviours and actions. The accent is on discovering what was experienced by an individual, rather than with questions surrounding why this or that happened. In one sense, this connects to the interest in the topic of consciousness, which was an important feature of the psychology of William James and others in the earliest days of the discipline. However, with phenomenological research in psychology the 'stuff' of consciousness is not the focal point. Instead, the researcher is interested in the individual's description of how some 'thing' was experienced. In this way, the phenomenologist would argue it is possible to deal with consciousness since consciousness does not exist as some independent reality, but is always directed at a particular event or thing.

This difficult and easily misunderstood distinction between other qualitative approaches and phenomenology has led some to argue that the differences between the two are insignificant and unimportant (Spinelli, 1989). An example may highlight that the difference between each, is in fact considerable. Investigating the feelings of isolation associated with the experience of a career ending injury in sport, could involve an attempt to get the individual to describe how the event has altered their lives and how they are trying to cope with its impact on their career in sport. This could lead to a rich, in-depth and detailed qualitative account of how the injury happened, how they felt about it and what sorts of challenges they were now facing as a result. In contrast, with the phenomenological approach, the psychological researcher is required to concentrate only on getting the injured sports person to describe their thoughts and feelings in relation to the injury, without attempting to examine its causes or the possible ways to deal with it. It is as though the injury can be dealt with by the researcher and the injured person *apart* from any awareness of what the likely implications could be for someone in this situation. Whilst very difficult to achieve, all efforts are directed at staying true to the pure description of the raw meaning of the injury for the person, without slipping into some kind of explanation or analysis of the event. Phenomenology requires the researcher and the subject to maintain their penetrating gaze at the phenomenon under consideration, *without* moving off target and starting to try and *account* for its existence or to speculate on its future impact.

The phenomenological method

In order to investigate particular events from a phenomenological base, the nineteenth century philosopher, Husserl, developed a precise method. Phenomenological method requires the researcher or therapist to, 'set aside our "natural attitude" – that objects in the external world are objectively present in space and time – and instead focus solely on our immediate and present experiencing of them' (Cooper, 2003: 10). The first stage in following this method requires the use of what has been called, *the rule of epoché*. This term literally means that the person must attempt to reduce their biases by a suspension of belief in everything that is not actually experienced. This process, which is referred to as *bracketing*, is meant to allow for a more direct focus on the 'what' of an experience itself. The idea is to reduce the influence of expectations, personal bias and our preconceived views. According to Spinelli (1996), this is so that we are able to be more confident that we are getting a truthful account of an event or a person's experience. A further check on the validity of any interpretation of data provided by the person is recommended, through allowing them to confirm the accuracy of any subsequent written account provided by the researcher or psychologist.

It is accepted that the process of bracketing can never be complete. However, the aim is to do as much as can be done to remove as many obstacles as possible to be able to achieve a direct engagement with a particular phenomenon. In summarizing the most important aspects of this method, Cohn (1997: 11) states that the aim is 'to describe, as far as possible, the intentional experience as uncontaminated by foreknowledge, bias and explanation'.

The second stage in applying the phenomenological method is to focus on description. The person is encouraged to describe an event or experience usually through use of a phenomenological interview. This consists of a more naturalistic style of questioning, which is often presented in an open-ended and non-standardized way. In his clear and impressive account of phenomenological interviewing in sport psychology, Dale (1996) suggests that the interview is more like a conversation. The intention is to reduce any perceived hierarchical barriers between the researcher and the person being interviewed. When this is achieved, the research interview is almost identical to the existential encounter (described in Chapter 5). This clearly places very different demands on the researcher utilizing the phenomenological method. For example, they must engage in the spontaneous, passionate and emotional experience, which a conversation with another person on personally significant events often involves. However, they must not totally abandon themselves to this mode of communication throughout the phenomenological interview. This is because although the researcher should approach the other person as a *co-researcher* (Giorgi, 1970) and therefore as an equal, they must from time-to-time step back and provide some structure to the process as well! The most obvious examples of this relate to the need to record data (if written) in sessions and to meet particular time constraints.

At a more 'psychological' level it is important to accept that as Buber (1958) has pointed out, whilst there is a great deal that can be achieved through losing oneself in a deep level of dialogue with another person, there is much to be gained by communicating from a more distant position. Although Buber's thoughts on this are most often used to explain the nature of an encounter within an existential approach, arguably they are equally relevant within the phenomenological interview. He describes in profound and powerful terms how empathy and genuine dialogue with another are central to authentic communication. In relation to empathy, he says that:

The psychotherapist, like the educator, must stand again and again not merely at his own pole in the bipolar relation, but also with the strength of present realization at the other pole, and experience the effect of his own action.

(Buber, 1958: 166)

Nevertheless, there exists a dynamic and creative tension between the researcher and a co-researcher during a phenomenological interview that is impossible to avoid or remove. Buber argues that this situation actually enhances the process of psychotherapy because:

Healing, like education, is only possible to the one who lives over against the other, and yet is detached ... Every I–Thou relationship, within a relation which is specified as a purposive working of one part upon the other, persists in virtue of a mutuality which is forbidden to be full.

(Buber, 1958: 167)

This view could be extended to the phenomenological interview and is helpful at highlighting differences with other methods within the qualitative research paradigm. In other words, the fact that there can never be complete and total equality between the co-researcher and the researcher is actually something that can have a positive effect. Buber is arguing that at the margins as it were, between two persons engaged in dialogue, there must exist a power differential where one individual has the responsibility to guide the process. He is claiming that an abdication of this role is not only impossible in practice but would reduce the encounter or research interview to merely a conversation.

According to Spinelli (1989), the final stage in applying the phenomenological method is referred to as the rule of *equalization*. This requires the phenomenologist to encourage the co-researcher to describe the components of an experience without attempting to order these in any particular way. Both the researcher and co-researcher within the interview are to resist the temptation to employ:

Any hierarchical assumptions with regard to the items of description ... to treat each bit of initial experience as if we have been given the task of piecing together some gigantic jigsaw puzzle without the prior knowledge of what the completed puzzle depicts.

(Spinelli, 1989: 19)

Given this, it is easier to see one of the clear differences between the phenomenological method and other qualitative approaches. For example, most qualitative research methods attempt to investigate both the feelings associated with an experience or event and the subject or participant's understanding of it. Questions aimed at explaining how something was understood by someone introduces an analytical, detached perspective and leads to a focus on why a thing happened. This is very difficult to avoid because in many ways it parallels how we talk with one another in our ordinary lives.

With the phenomenological method, the focus is on providing an experiential account alone; no attempt must be made during the interview to interpret, re-order or analyse the descriptive material. Although difficult to achieve, the challenge is to focus on what the co-researcher says related to a lived-experience and to avoid reference to theories or hypothesis to guide the dialogue or to provide a framework for data analysis. This objection to the use of theory is because these formulations and the conceptualizing and hypothesizing which are integral to them are abstractions, and do not directly relate to the everyday real world. Existential phenomenologists tend to reject the use of theory and concepts outright because as Ihde (1986: 34) sharply expresses it, their message is, '*Describe, don't explain*'.

Phenomenological research in sport

In terms of collecting interview data, checks on validity, research procedures, design and presentation of results, there is considerable overlap between phenomenological method and other qualitative methods. Within sport psychology research Dale (1996, 2000) has outlined, in clear and easy to follow terms, the steps involved in data analysis according to the phenomenological method. Whilst there are several ways in which data can be dealt with and presented in this approach, much of what Dale suggests would be quite familiar to most qualitative researchers. He describes how after transcribing each interview, a process was followed involving a group of phenomenological researchers establishing clusters of themes based on their agreed interpretations of the meaning phrases and statements within the transcripts. Efforts were made to employ the sports participant's language in the interpretations which were carried out at both the idiographic and nomothetic levels. At the end of this process, the researcher then returns to the co-researchers and asks them to assess the descriptions relating to their experience. Finally, Dale (2000) states that any changes to the text suggested by the individual co-researchers are included in the final document. This process attempts to ensure that the participant's account of an experience in their own language remains visible throughout all levels of data analysis. The most important check on the validity of this approach is that the first person description of the phenomenon must be clearly and constantly articulated at all stages (Giorgi, 1970).

Results of studies using the phenomenological method may be presented in a number of ways. Again, these include those which are currently extensively used within other qualitative research in sport psychology. For example, Dale's (2000) study of elite decathletes utilized a thematic analysis and included detailed excerpts from the phenomenologically derived accounts provided by each of the seven performers. This structuring and re-ordering of the material provided by the athletes during their interviews is allowable within this approach. However, it should be recalled that any such input from the researcher is not acceptable during the data gathering stage (i.e. interviews). The use of thematic analysis to codify data and display results prior to an in-depth discussion of them has been used quite extensively in sport psychology research during the past ten years. The work of Gould *et al.* (1993) investigating the experience of stress with national level skaters was one of the earliest to use thematic analysis, although this study did not rely on a phenomenological approach.

Finally, before attempting to summarize the key elements in this approach and discuss some of its drawbacks, there are two further important (if somewhat difficult to understand) issues to consider. First, phenomenology rests on the idea that our minds are not passive receivers of stimuli, but that we are always involved in the process by which we designate something as a particular object or thing. This is captured by the term, *intentionality*; it refers to the fact that following Brentano (the originator of this idea), the 'real physical world exists outside our consciousness and that, as such all consciousness is always directed towards the real world in order to interpret it in a meaningful manner' (Spinelli, 1989: 11). Of course, given that we can never completely separate ourselves from this act of perceiving things in the world, it becomes impossible to bracket this as can be attempted with the particular biases and preconceived ideas we bring with us. Although some phenomenologists adopt the view that reality is all in our minds, others, following Brentano, Marcel and Roberts see it differently. They accept that it is true to say that we can only ever see things through our interpretations of them. They point out that the question of whether things really exist independently of our minds is a philosophical question. Fortunately, the phenomenological method can often be applied without having to choose between these two counter views.

There are undoubtedly some occasions, where a choice must be made between these competing positions. For example, where phenomenological studies are looking at the individual's experiences surrounding the interpretation of values or the meaning of life and spiritual matters, the differences could be very profound. Following one approach would necessarily lead to a perspective where values would be relative, and the ultimate meaning of life could only be my view and not one related to some pre-established system of beliefs. In contrast, for the phenomenological psychologist operating within the tradition of Marcel and the others, my experience in relation to describing the issue of values, or other significant personal areas of life, will provide data which cannot be portrayed as anything other than my views and therefore as restricted accounts by the fact of my subjectivity as a human person. In other words, these experiential accounts are just that and nothing else according to this view. By being psychological and individual, they cannot be elevated to represent the truth about reality because this is not a power given to them. This issue has been discussed earlier in the chapter. Although very difficult to articulate, it remains the main point of disagreement between those who see existentialism and phenomenology in terms of freedom detached from any foundations, and the earlier group for whom liberation can only mean something in relation to a *reality that precedes it* – which is always there.

The second important foundational notion relating to the phenomenological method is that of *noema* and *noesis*. The *noetic* element refers to the person's thinking and emotional biases which add meaning to some 'thing' beyond its content. The *noematic* dimension is formed by the information or content which is associated with an experience. For example, the noise made by a football crowd cannot be understood by its content (i.e. the words shouted and chants) alone but only alongside an individual's experience of this. The football fan may experience something very different to the police officer on duty at the match! The noematic focus relates to questions of what and the noetic element is captured by questions addressing how an experience is encountered.

Summary of the phenomenological method

Husserl (1970) has pointed out that different methodologies can be considered phenomenological however, all are interested in accessing and describing pure phenomena prior to scientific interpretation. The focus is not on the world described, interpreted and created by scientific fact, but on the world of everyday experience. The phenomenological method allows us to contact phenomena as we actually live them out and experience them. In the natural science approach, referred to as the *natural attitude* (Giorgi, 1970), something is understood and explained by an outside observer acting objectively. In contrast, with the phenomenological approach empathic understanding is required to enable someone to come to a partial understanding of another person's behaviour. Given this, it is easy to see the connection with existentialism. Both phenomenology and existential psychology are more interested in the experience of the individual rather than groups, since they argue that each person is unique. Therefore, a reductionist approach which is oriented towards the study of groups and categories of people is not appropriate, although, phenomenologists will offer general statements based on commonalities that emerge from their idiographic analysis.

Although not primarily addressing the place of phenomenology within psychology, Csikszentmihalyi (1992) has claimed that the most dominant models and approaches have been reductionist, mechanistic and more about pathology than positive experiences. Although positive psychology seems to be beginning to establish itself (Seligman and Csikszentmihalyi, 2000), very few seem aware that phenomenology could provide a method which would allow researchers to investigate consciousness itself. This area of psychology has been studied from a neuro-physiological perspective and directly through the work of William James and the introspectionists in the nineteenth century. However, both of these approaches to the study of consciousness are shot through with serious epistemonological and methodological problems, not the least of which is that consciousness, as Chesterton (1910) wryly noted about education, refers to a *process* and not a thing as such. This ephemeral quality of consciousness and the diffi-culty of measuring it, has increasingly led psychology off in other directions. Although the British Psychological Society has recently established a section on consciousness and experiential psychology, the discipline of psychology and much of sport psychology, remain wedded to a particular outlook. In attempting to discuss the reasons for this state of affairs one prolific researcher and writer has had this to say:

> The major psychological trends of this century including drive theories, psychoanalysis, behaviourism, cognitive psychology, and the contemporary atheoretical neuropharmacological approaches – all share a common epis-temology. In an attempt to be as scientific as possible, they have developed reductionistic accounts of human action, discounting or ignoring the most obvious aspect of human phenomenon, namely, the existence of a con-scious self.
>
> (Csikszentmihalyi, 1988: 15)

According to Polkinghorne (1989), phenomenological methods in psychology could help overcome some of these failings in traditional psychology and sport psychology because they aim to investigate the area between human conscious-ness and the world around us. This zone is human experience and can be studied scientifically where we follow the stages contained within the phenome-nological method – the rule of epoché, allowing data to emerge spontaneously, use of bracketing and reliance on the descriptions provided by the person them-selves. Phenomenological sport psychology would be interested in producing ever more adequate and complete accounts of our experience of the world. This would lead to a more thorough analysis of how each person, as a unique indi-vidual, experiences both commonly shared factors, which nevertheless are clothed in a singular and personal set of meanings. For example, anxiety before a major personal challenge is a universally experienced phenomenon. However, how that emotion is encountered and what it means to each person is some-thing only they can articulate with any validity.

Giorgi (1985) suggests that to facilitate the collection of this kind of data studies should use open-ended questions and work with research participants who do not have any knowledge of the researcher's biases and theoretical orien-tation. Van Kaam (1969) has stressed that this type of research requires study participants or co-researchers to possess several skills such as, the ability to communicate effectively, to discuss feelings and emotions without inhibition, and to be able to go beyond this to a more embodied and holistic account of an experience. The phenomenological interview could then proceed as something very close to the existential psychology encounter. The session would involve deep interpersonal communication and an attempt to allow for spontaneous dialogue whilst maintaining focus on the experience to be described. Data is then written up by the researcher who will show this in turn to the study participants to check for validity of any summary, themes and interpretations.

The final aim of the research is to reveal the basic and central structure of the experience which has been studied.

This brief description of the steps involved in data-generation and analysis in phenomenological psychology, highlights some of the difficulties associated with this approach. First, it could be argued that the research participants need a considerable number of skills and a high level of awareness and self-knowledge. This would mean that for many individuals, such as children, those with poor oral and verbal skills and people who are uncomfortable discussing their experiences with relative strangers, the phenomenological approach may be very difficult to use. In terms of the phenomenological interview, the researcher must be able to 'throw themselves into an encounter' with another person, maintain a focus on what is being described by the study participant, whilst also seeking to constantly clarify what is being said. Such a demanding task may be off putting to many less experienced researchers or those lacking confidence in their interpersonal skills.

Second, the requirement to focus on questions of what and how, and not why, may be very difficult to achieve for researchers trained in the natural scientific approach in psychology and sport psychology. The temptation to 'take over' the interview and to ignore the need to let the data emerge more or less spontaneously represents a significant challenge for researchers more used to collecting data through more closed, forced and directive means.

Third, the process involved in providing an analysis of the interview data is time consuming and requires considerable writing skills. The stages or steps in this have been described comprehensively by Van Kaam (1969), Colaizzi (1978) and more recently in sport psychology by Dale (1996, 2000). These accounts convey that this demands both technical skill and a feeling for the process overall; this more artistic element relies on intuition, imagination and the ability to sense what is being described. The final part of the analysis involves an attempt to translate the descriptions, themes, and meaning units provided by the participant into a synthesis containing both psychological terms and everyday language. This is made even more arduous because as Polkinghorne (1989) has pointed out, the psychological terms used must be those from phenomenological psychology. However, because of the history and development of psychology and sport psychology, most researchers are tied to terminology and concepts which have their roots in behaviourism, psychoanalysis or cognitive psychology.

Conclusion

The phenomenological interview allows individuals to describe their experiences in rich detail, and can provide researchers and applied practitioners with information that might be impossible to access in any other way. Within sport psychology, several experienced applied consultants (Nesti and Sewell, 1997; Ravizza, 2002) have advocated that to be effective, MST programmes must be individualized to meet an athlete's needs. The phenomenological method allows for this through its concern with what an athlete experiences and enables these accounts to be used by other sports performers as part of their mental preparation. Dale's (2000) study of the lived experience of elite decathletes identified that despite bringing their own personal meanings to the descriptions of their most memorable performances, the thematic analysis was able to reveal commonalities among them as a group. Again, this highlights that phenomenology is able to combine both idiographic and nomothetic approaches to data analysis to give a more complete perspective on a specific event.

Finally, the worth of this approach may be tested in relation to its capacity to generate findings that can shape future policy and practice in psychology and sport psychology. This ultimate assessment of validity is especially important with phenomenological research because of the claims of phenomenological philosophy and psychology. According to Giorgi (1985), it is concerned with generating descriptive data, based solely on a person's experience. This is then thematized and structured and; 'In those cases where the phenomenon is one that the readers have experienced, the findings must also correspond to the readers' own experiences of the phenomenon' (Polkinghorne, 1989: 57).

The phenomenological approach can be used to investigate a wide range of traditional psychological areas. Studies have considered the experience of various emotions, perception, learning, memory, child development and most other topics in psychology. Within sport and exercise psychology, fewer studies employing phenomenological methods have been carried out. Fahlberg *et al.* (1992) looked at exercise from an existential phenomenological perspective and Dale (1996, 2000) has utilized a phenomenological interview method in his work with sports performers. More recently, Kerry and Armour (2000) discussed how phenomenology could be used to improve understanding within the sports sciences. A number of researchers within sport psychology have also utilized phenomenological methods to explore the use of Christian prayer in sport (Czech *et al.*, 2004), the phenomena of sport (Johnson and Butryn, 2002) and the experience of athlete transition and change (Molnar, 2002). In terms of the place of spirituality in sport psychology, Nesti (2004) has argued that:

> Phenomenology provides a particularly suitable and appropriate method for collecting data from the athletes' 'lived world.'

Finally, phenomenology may be a useful approach for understanding the challenges associated with transition and phases of significant change. Yalom (1999) refers to these as *boundary situations*. Within sport, this could be used to describe experiences such as career termination, retirement or being moved onto a different level or team. These and other similar situations are likely to be accompanied by feelings of normal anxiety. A phenomenological account of experiences may help sports performers and researchers in sport psychology to gain a more complete and personal account of important moments in an athlete's life. This in turn could be used to help applied sport psychologists by increasing their understanding and knowledge of the real world faced by their client-athletes.

4 Anxiety and sport

An existential-phenomenological approach

Introduction

Existential psychology like other approaches in psychology is concerned with investigating all of the moods and emotions experienced by people in their lives. This includes what have been referred to by others as positive affect and negative affect, (Watson and Tellegen, 1985) and positive and negative mood states (McNair *et al.*, 1971). However, the strict distinction between positive and negative feelings and emotions is less important to the existential psychologist because they are not interested in identifying mental states as such; their focus is directed at revealing what a particular mental experience means to a person. This of course is consistent with the underlying holistic viewpoint of existential-phenomenological psychology, where interest is on what the person describes rather than which mood state or emotion the researcher or therapist wishes to measure. Existentialism emphasizes that since we rarely, if ever, experience pure and discrete categories of positive or negative feelings, it is important that we view human emotion and mood as something which cannot be understood apart from our whole being; it is not possible to look at it as one could analyse some 'thing' which exists *beyond ourselves*. Finally, and most controversially, existential psychology claims that it is more helpful to recognize that the most important psychological fact of the human condition is that we experience anxiety throughout the whole of our lives and that how we deal with this influences how much joy or despair we encounter.

In his review of the major theories of anxiety, Fischer (1970) suggests that the concept of anxiety holds a central position in most psychological approaches. Freudians and other psychologists have tended to view anxiety as a uniformly negative emotional state. According to Caruso (1964), interest has been aimed largely at techniques and strategies for controlling or removing the sensation of anxiety. However, in almost complete contrast, therapists and researchers following various existential and phenomenologically based approaches, such as Fromm (1994) and Schneider and May (1995), offer a more complex and less negative account of anxiety and its function. In general, they view anxiety as a universal phenomenon featuring throughout the lives of all individuals irrespective of their psychological condition or health. This perspective tends to emphasize the potential for anxiety to be viewed favourably by individuals and at least, not always described as a debilitating feature which must be avoided.

However, research in sport has tended to conceptualize anxiety as a debilitative emotion. Following the earlier work of Spielberger (1966), anxiety has been divided into state and trait dimensions. The anxiety response has been considered in terms of cognitive and somatic subcomponents (Davidson and Schwartz, 1976). This multidimensional approach to anxiety has been further developed by Martens *et al.* (1990) in sport. According to Martens, the most influential approaches in sport psychology, especially in English speaking countries, have been cognitive psychology and trait psychology. Investigations into anxiety and sport have, as a result, most usually involved the study of groups and the use of psychometric tests, such as the SCAT (Martens, 1977) and the CSAI-2 (Martens *et al.*, 1990).

In common with earlier work in the mainstream, sports researchers have begun to highlight problems associated with viewing anxiety only as a destructive emotion. A series of studies (Jones *et al.*, 1994; Edwards and Hardy, 1996) have revealed that anxiety, can on occasion, be seen as facilitative of good performance by some athletes, and that this directional element may be a more important predictor of success, than intensity or level of anxiety.

A considerable difficulty remains that the majority of studies aimed at investigating anxiety in sport have focused on pre-competition anxiety levels and only recently on athletes' perceptions surrounding these. Arguably, many of the findings to date have been largely predictable and somewhat mundane. A basic understanding of sports performance and competitive sport reveals that athletes often get more nervous closer to the event and that experienced performers or those with high self-confidence tend to be less concerned about their anxiety levels before competition. In addition, anecdotal accounts and interviews indicate that athletes often feel good, or at least are quite neutral, about their feelings of anxiety prior to an event. For many sport psychologists working with athletes, it could be argued that much of the empirically based research, to date, into anxiety and sport is of little practical use. There are researchers such as Jones (1995: 469), who have defended this position by reminding us that 'sport psychology is not merely about practical issues'. Jones has highlighted that there has been a general failure in efforts aimed at predicting performance variance from pre-competitive anxiety measures. This has been frequently explained as due to the inappropriate performance measures used in some studies, and that 'performance as an ongoing process across time' (Edwards and Hardy, 1996: 307) would represent a more sound approach to measurement.

However, the relatively few studies which have been able to clearly identify a link between anxiety and sports performance may be taken as yet further evidence that existing approaches to the study of anxiety in sport lack ecological validity. For example, most studies have restricted themselves to assessing precompetition anxiety intensity (and direction), although in the vast majority of sports, anxiety in-event is likely to be more important in influencing performance. Recent work by Jones *et al.* (1997) has begun to investigate the experience of in-event anxiety and its relation to performance; this is a welcome development although again the tendency is to view anxiety as generally a negative emotional state. It may be argued that it is equally likely that no such clear relationship actually exists between anxiety and sports performance and that as Gill (1994) has suggested, a much broader range of constructs need to be considered if researchers are to be able to begin to seriously address this issue. Interestingly, the individualized zone of optimal functioning hypothesis (IZOF) considers that each athlete possesses an optimal level across a range of emotional states including anxiety where sports performance will be superior (Hanin and Syrja, 1995). IZOF represents a very promising addition to work in this area because of its idiographic basis, and it stresses that anxiety is best understood alongside and in relation to a broad range of other important emotions.

All of this highlights that the view taken by existential psychology towards anxiety is closer to some of the more recent approaches to its study in sport psychology. Nevertheless, the existential account of anxiety remains very different to those provided in other schools of psychology. The implications of following this approach for both research and practice in sport psychology are many; the most important of these will now be considered and suggestions made relating to possible future developments, which is argued are necessary if anxiety in sport is to be understood in a way that more closely connects to how it is experienced by those involved in sport.

Competitive anxiety and sport

In his comprehensive and impressive review of competitive anxiety research in sport, Jones has offered the following observations:

> Like anxiety researchers in other areas of psychology, sport psychologists have wrestled with the conceptual and methodological dilemmas surrounding examination of the anxiety response itself ... [and that,] research into the anxiety sports performance relationship, in particular, has served to increase knowledge of a complex phenomenon which has sometimes proved somewhat elusive to examine in some other situational contexts.
>
> (Jones, 1995: 450)

The above statements by one of the most prolific researchers of anxiety and sport in recent years, seem to suggest that research in this area has built up a solid body of work based on conceptual clarity and has provided a more complete understanding of the phenomenon of anxiety. However, this level of optimism is not shared by all, especially those such as Fahlberg *et al.* (1992) and Dale (2000), who have pointed out that the dominant reductionist paradigm of general psychology has held an exclusive and almost unassailable position in sport psychology. This situation they have argued, has led to a narrow focus where psychological investigation has been solely concerned with identifying causes of behaviour and has eschewed interest in exploring the meaning associated with such behaviours. The practical effects of this are clearly evident in the dearth of studies that have investigated the meaning of anxiety for an individual athlete. There have been few attempts at using qualitative methodologies (Dale, 2000) or alternative approaches (Gould *et al.*, 1993) in the study of stress and anxiety in sport.

Whilst Jones (1995: 469) has suggested that more focus should be devoted 'to examine both the concept and the construct of competitive anxiety', arguably there remains much confusion within the sport extant literature. Stress, arousal and even fear and anxiety have been used as though each describes the same emotion. In addition, stress and anxiety have been typically viewed as negative states, which seems contrary to Selye's (1956) original account of stress as an essentially neutral phenomenon, which can be experienced positively as *Eustress* or negatively as distress.

This overwhelming tendency to consider stress and anxiety as negative emotions has in turn led to a plethora of studies aimed at investigating stress management and anxiety control in sport. A further feature of this perspective is that few published studies on competitive anxiety in sport fail to conclude that their results suggest that specific behavioural or more clearly psychological techniques can be used by athletes to overcome the supposed adverse effects of anxiety on sports performance, even where there is little empirical support for this. Having begun in a modest fashion to explore group differences and report interesting correlations, it seems rather surprising and flagrantly unscientific to specify particular actions where cause and effect has not been 'proved' or subjected to any real scrutiny! Fortunately, there are some important examples of where this pitfall has been avoided (Gould *et al.*, 1993; Dale, 2000); these studies tend to leave the issue of interventions and cure alone, and focus more properly on attempting to describe the experience of stress and anxiety for individual athletes or groups of athletes.

In conclusion, the narrowness of much of the work investigating anxiety and sport was noted by Jones and Hardy (1990) over a decade ago. They called for a much greater use of alternative methodologies to be used in future studies. However, a survey of their extensive and highly respected research in the area since that time, and most of the work of others, reveals that it has largely failed to address this issue. It could be argued that a major shift to consider other methodologies and methods is unlikely to occur without renewed focus on the conceptualizations of anxiety. In terms of providing for sound and clear conceptual distinctions between anxiety and stress, the answer may lie in revisiting older and more developed schools of psychological theory, especially those with definitions and descriptions of anxiety and stress which provide an unambiguous differentiation between these two concepts.

An existential account of anxiety

Existential-phenomenological psychology is based on existentialism, a formal philosophical school which seeks to understand an individual's concrete, lived situation; to achieve this, focus is directed at the meaning that an event has for a particular person.

The apparent fuzziness of the terms used in existential-phenomenological psychology in particular, and that the philosophical roots are to be found in mainland Europe (especially in Germany and France during the nineteenth century), goes some way to explaining why little was known of this approach to psychology in North America until May introduced it in 1950 (deCarvalho, 1996). May's PhD dissertation on 'The Meaning of Anxiety', considered the subject by drawing on theory from a number of schools of psychology, however, it was the first time that an American had provided an in-depth account of anxiety from an existential psychology perspective. Of considerable importance for existential psychology is the distinction between what May (1977) refers to as normal anxiety and neurotic anxiety. This view contends that normal anxiety is not disproportionate to an objective threat, involves little repression and can be dealt with constructively. Neurotic anxiety however, is more of a problem according to this view as it involves repression, a disproportionate reaction to a threat, and often results in various inhibitions and a closing up of the personality. Thus, researchers and clinicians supporting this interpretation of anxiety believe that only a particular type of anxiety, that is neurotic, is problematic for the individual. In addition, May (1977) states that neurotic anxiety occurs when a person has failed repeatedly to meet the challenge of normal anxiety. This view strongly suggests that strategies and techniques should not be aimed at the removal or elimination of anxiety, as normal anxiety is healthy in that it is associated with personal growth and is something which all individuals experience.

Interestingly, existential-phenomenological psychology has tended to focus on anxiety rather than stress and has typically described the anxiety state as involving diffuse apprehension. In contrast, fear is viewed as a psychological and behavioural reaction to a specific object of danger, whilst anxiety involves a vague feeling, even though as May has pointed out, 'anxiety may be more painful than fear' (May, 1977: 181).

A major misunderstanding, it has been argued (Valle *et al.*, 1989), has held back the acceptance of existential psychology into the mainstream. Existential psychology is not purely subjective or introspectionist, and according to Valle and Halling, it represents more of a middle ground between purely objective and purely subjective approaches. The major interest of existential-phenomenological psychology is to reveal the meaning of form, or expressed differently – to investigate the structure of experience. Within sport psychology, the few largely qualitative studies in stress and anxiety (Ming and Martin, 1996) are typically less interested in the structure or meaning of these terms for individual athletes. Valle *et al.* (1989) have pointed out that qualitative research in psychology often remains attached to the philosophical assumptions of the dominant, natural scientific orthodoxy of mechanical determinism, where all events are viewed in terms of a strict cause and effect relationship. This bias, although rarely reflected upon openly in most sport psychology research, can even be clearly discerned within apparently radical and alternative research methodologies, such as those relying on single subject designs.

For example, Ming and Martin's (1996) study on the use of self-talk packages in skating revealed that a single subject design, utilizing objective behavioural observation and self-reports enabled the researchers to confirm that self-talk was used to improve performance. In supporting this finding, Ming and Martin (1996: 235) have claimed that their 'experimental design indicates that the improvements were due to the treatment package and not to some uncontrollable variable'. However, such dogmatic and unswerving confidence in the power of traditional experimental studies in being able to isolate cause and effect, is rarely to be found, even in modern physics according to Giorgi (1970). He has suggested that the rigour of natural science may be more apparent than real when the underlying metaphysical and technical assumptions are exposed. In calling for a *human science* approach to psychology, he has advocated that the excessive and almost blind adherence to natural science approaches are unlikely to furnish any truly important or significant findings; especially given that humans are always both the objects and the subjects of inquiry.

The hegemony of the natural science approach to psychology (Rennie, 1994) both in research and in practice, has as yet, been largely unrecognized in sport and exercise psychology. Although Fahlberg *et al.*'s (1992) work in exercise psychology and Dale's (1996) and Corlett's (1996) in sport psychology has begun to address some related issues. In conclusion, it may be that the fracture between the findings of most sport psychology research into anxiety, and the everyday understanding of the experience of anxiety and performance in sport, may not be healed by persisting with an approach which seems to have very rarely offered any new and exciting discoveries.

By investigating the meaning of anxiety in sport, rather than trying to identify its cause or supposed effect on performance, researchers may be able to develop links with other related and important topics in sport psychology. For example, both Jackson and Csikszentmihalyi's (1999) work on the Flow model, and Kerr's (1997) research on metamotivational states, anxiety and arousal, bring anxiety and motivation together by focusing on how these constructs influence and shape one another. That these dynamic and broader views of anxiety are presented in Csikszentmihalyi's and Kerr's work has much to do with the phenomenological and existential focus of Flow theory and Reversal theory.

In fact, even earlier support for the existential account of anxiety emerged from the work of White (1959) on the concept of competence. He described how researchers from experimental laboratory based psychology and those espousing psychoanalytic ego psychology, concluded that anxiety reduction was the central motive in the development of an effective ego. However, White's work challenged the ascendancy of this view and suggested that rather than avoiding anxiety and novelty, much behaviour is motivated by an attempt to experience raised tension, stimulation and variety. In practical life, this 'master motive', which produces feelings of efficacy in an individual, can be seen in the exploratory play of children, and adult engagement in challenging and goal directed behaviour such as competitive sport and exercise programmes. Although the main focus of his work was to question the supremacy of drive-reduction theory and psychoanalytic instinct theory, the implications for anxiety research were considerable. Taken as a whole, White's important work on motivation highlights that there are instances where anxiety is actually sought out and that as Kierkegaard (1844/1944) has argued, *anxiety becomes the great teacher!*

Kierkegaard has been highlighted by Fischer (1970) as the person most often identified as the founder of modern existential philosophy and psychology and the first to consider the nature of anxiety in his book, *The Concept of Dread* (1844). Of major significance to sport psychology, Kierkegaard maintained that anxiety is both part of and a requirement for the growth of a person, or as he terms it, *a self*. He advocated that by facing up to and moving through anxiety, the individual is better prepared to face the experience of anxiety again. As this process is repeated throughout life, individuals teach themselves faith and courage, and will be able to face their freedom and life, rather than devoting their energies to evading anxiety experiences. This description of anxiety explains why, according to the existentialists, anxiety can have a positive function, and that anxiety accompanies life where the person accepts personal responsibility for their decisions and actions.

It may be suggested that, rather than follow Martens *et al.*'s (1990) ultimately limited and narrow approach to competitive anxiety research in sport, a much better response would have been to return to the much earlier and more comprehensive theories of anxiety provided by Freud, Jung and the existential psychologists. That these different approaches in psychology view anxiety as of considerable importance can be gauged from Freud's comments that, 'the problem of anxiety is a nodal point at which the most various and important questions converge, a riddle whose solution would be bound to throw a flood of light upon our whole mental existence' (Freud, 1991: 393).

Freud, it seems, considered anxiety to be something affecting all human beings and was interested in explaining why some people experienced more of it than others. His interest and that of his followers was on identifying the causes of anxiety. This he did by referring to underlying energy systems, and by describing the tensions arising out of the interplay between the three psychic processes of the id, ego and superego, and the external world. However, in keeping with the natural scientific model, little attention was directed at the meaning of anxiety.

In contrast, and in radical opposition to this, existential psychologists following Kierkegaard and May have been almost exclusively interested in the individual's experience of anxiety and largely uninterested in its causes. Although still one-sided in its focus, following this approach to anxiety would have likely resulted in research findings of greater ecological validity.

Identification of the causes of anxiety in sport and its meaning could be given considerable impetus by recognition of what May (1977) has termed normal anxiety and neurotic anxiety. Although these constructs have been discussed earlier, it is worth reiterating that neurotic anxiety, according to the existential psychologists, is the problem and that normal anxiety is not. The sports literature has focused almost exclusively on the symptoms of anxiety following Spielberger's multidimensional model. Such a view of course has little to say about the potentially positive aspect of anxiety, and crudely proceeds from the assumption that anxiety is rather like illness in that one suffers from it and would never actively seek it out. However, competitive sport is a stressful activity and anxiety is experienced in it on occasion. Put simply, if anxiety is so bad, why do so many people engage freely and often for no obvious extrinsic reward in such a potentially anxiety inducing pursuit as competitive sport? A fuller explanation of this must surely draw on the idea of normal anxiety being that anxiety which we are prepared to experience and even enjoy. Kierkegaard has managed to catch this apparently paradoxical aspect of anxiety by describing it as an experience which accompanies something that we simultaneously fear and yet desire. In straightforward terms, we often find ourselves genuinely anxious prior to a task which often involves some considerable discomfort and yet be prepared to meet the challenge, especially where we feel competent and the activity is more or less freely chosen. Some theorists have described this emotional state as not in fact anxiety, but excitement. However, it could be argued whilst positive anxiety is more likely another name for excitement, that normal anxiety can be experienced (usually before and during the event) as a beneficial and facilitative experience is to say something quite different.

Coaches and others have frequently been denigrated for using so called 'psyching up' tactics to induce greater anxiety in their players prior to an event. It seems that they believe in the galvanizing effects of normal anxiety on performance; although, sports researchers are only now beginning to seriously consider this in their work. In supporting this point, Schneider and May (1995) reported that many psychologists in the mainstream agree that anxiety facilitates performance up to a certain point and that beyond this level performance may decline. However, they cite the much earlier important work of Denny (1966), which explains performance deterioration in terms of poor preparation or lack of ability, rather than anxiety. That anxiety is the result of poor performance, or the anticipation that one will perform unsuccessfully because of a lack of ability or inadequate preparation, seems a very likely explanation of much of the test anxiety research findings, which report that poor performance is strongly associated with anxiety. In sport, the knowledge that an individual has not trained properly, or lacks the sufficient skill or ability to succeed, surely represents the more likely explanation of the hypothesized strong relationship between high levels of anxiety and poor performance.

In summary, the answer would seem to already lie elsewhere and yet sport psychology appears determined to follow approaches that have been of little success in the mainstream in the past. One notable and disturbing example is the recent interest shown in psycho-physiological approaches to anxiety in sport. Jones (1995) has advocated that this approach is worthy of being pursued, although May warned many years earlier that without an integrating theory of mind–body, three common errors would continue to plague research in this area:

> The first is the error, on the one side, of identifying an emotion with a neurophysiological process. The second is the error in the middle of a 'neu-rologizing tautology' (e.g. merely describing sympathetic activity as the neurophysiological aspect of anxiety). And the third is the error on the other side of assuming a simple dichotomy between neurophysiological and psychological processes.
>
> (May, 1977: 94)

Sport anxiety research

Fischer (1970) has pointed out that the existential approach to anxiety could provide a more complete account of the phenomenon by including descriptions of the visible symptoms and behaviour of the anxious individual. This approach has been used in sports studies (Males and Kerr, 1996) where the subject has been shown a filmed recording of their performance and questioned on how they felt at different junctures. Although not addressing anxiety and perform-ance exclusively, this approach could have considerable potential in sports research, especially where studies are focusing on in-competition anxiety and its relationship to performance. For example, May's (1977) description of anxious experiencing describes how anxiety involves the catastrophic situation where an individual feels as though they are going to pieces. In addition, he has stated that we are able to observe certain changes in the physiognomy of a person experiencing anxiety, however, identification of causes can only begin to be achieved with any real accuracy by getting the subject to identify which causal agents make them feel anxious at any particular moment. In sport, a performer watching a recording of their own performance, may be able to explain that when they missed the penalty shot in a penalty shoot out, contrary to what might normally be expected, there was a sense of relief that their turn was over and that having done their best as a defender, it was now up to the strikers and attacking mid-fielders to make certain! In contrast, a striker may feel confident and largely anxiety free before their attempt and yet, upon scoring, start to experience anxiety because they have broken the flow and have now become aware of the importance of what they have just achieved (and consequently, what could have happened should they have missed). Alternatively, they may now experience intense competitive anxiety after their successful performance in relation to the performance of others (i.e. their team mates). An existential psychology based interpretation of this might focus on the distinction between successfully meeting a potentially anxiety-filled situation where the choice of action and responsibility was accepted. In contrast, where responsibility and control of events fall outside of an individual's influence, even though they have an acute and personal interest in the outcome, these may be occasions for the most debilitating and negatively perceived anxiety experiences.

It seems that a more complete understanding of anxiety in sport appears necessary before studies can attempt to identify and isolate causal relationships, even of a loose kind. Much more needs to be done to investigate the meaning of anxiety in sport for the individual athlete. Fischer's thorough review of the theories of anxiety put forward by all of the major schools of psychology, has pointed out that no single approach satisfactorily accounts for what he has termed, 'anxious experiencing and the experience of the other-being-anxious' (Fischer, 1970: 94). According to Fischer, most research has focused on assessing and measuring the *other-being-anxious* and apart from the approach of the existentialists, very little attention has been devoted to more subjective accounts of how anxiety is experienced by an individual themselves. The exclusive focus of the existentialists on the interpretation and meaning of anxiety for the individual could provide a much needed change of direction for sport anxiety research. The vast majority of studies so far have considered anxiety from the perspective of an observer.

Prior to assessing how such an integrated approach to anxiety would influence sports research, the following extensive quotation from Fischer seems to capture the essence of this new approach. In referring to the interpretation of the physiological symptoms of anxiety he contends that:

> All of the bodily phenomena that we have enumerated signify one and the same condition: my uncertain impotence and imminent collapse in the face of my crumbling world. Thus we can affirm with Schachter that different people manifest different bodily signs of anxiety: some express this condition through palpitations, others perspire, others tremble, etc. However, all of these bodily events have the same common experiential significance to the individuals undergoing them and only if the theoretician grasps the holistic character of human bodily functioning will he be able to realize that which the everyday individual already understands.
>
> (Fischer, 1970: 171)

Such a view clearly rejects the multidimensional models of anxiety as theoretical, abstract and of little practical use. Research based on multidimensional models would, according to this view, be unlikely to discover anything new about anxiety and sport, and be unable to offer any findings that could be of interest or help to coaches and their athletes. A review of the sport anxiety literature over the past two decades would largely support this conclusion, and yet sport psychologists and researchers continue to argue for more of the same. Instead, it is suggested that sport anxiety research will largely produce strikingly obvious and bland results and findings that continue to be ignored by sports practitioners, until it adopts different methodologies, methods and approaches to data analysis and interpretation. For the sake of consistency and scientific rigor, it could be argued that this realignment should be accompanied by explicit recognition that psychology (research) needs to proceed from a human science as opposed to a natural scientific approach (Giorgi, 1985). However, given that most researchers in sport psychology remain wedded to the meta-physical and philosophical assumptions of the natural scientific model, it may be too much to expect that many will be prepared to publicly renounce their beliefs. This could be particularly difficult as Rennie (1994) has argued that the dominant approach has been typically uncritically accepted and generally ignored as an issue by most sport anxiety researchers. More likely, recognition that much current work in the area has borne little fruit and is of even less interest to an increasingly vocal and important practically focused sports community should begin to broaden the approach taken towards sport anxiety research. The slight increase in the use of qualitative methodologies (Sparkes, 2002), greater calls for single subject design studies (Jones and Hardy, 1990) and for mood and emotion to be considered (Gill, 1994), suggest that sports researchers are slowly beginning to move closer towards a more ecologically valid and integrated approach to the study of anxiety.

Applied implications

It could be argued that the increasing activity of applied sport psychologists and the beginnings of some recognition of the need to do more than consider the athlete and their sport in isolation from the rest of daily life, will give impetus to greater use of qualitative research methodologies in sports research. In addition, this shift in emphasis to consider broader life issues facing the anxious athlete, should lead to an increasing acceptance that anxiety itself needs to be interpreted in relation to an individual's general mood states and emotion. This has been investigated in relation to positive and negative affect and competitive anxiety in sport by Jones *et al.* (1996).

A further promising development has been the work of Parkinson *et al.* in defining mood as, 'part of a broader system of action control and is itself subject to regulation in accordance with broader concerns relating to biology, culture, relationships and social and personal identity' (Parkinson *et al.*, 1996: 17). In attempting to differentiate mood from affect in general, it has been argued that mood lasts longer. It is generally held that emotion and emotional states refer to acute, brief or phasic episodes in comparison to the more tonic or chronic nature of mood. Again it has been postulated that 'mood is an undirected evaluative state which temporarily predisposes a person to interpret and act towards a wide variety of events in ways according with its affect content' (Parkinson *et al.*, 1996: 9–10). Emotion in contrast, may be understood as directed towards a specific object. This particular account of mood and emotion connects well with the approach taken by existential-phenomenological psychology in differentiating between anxiety and fear.

Although broadening sport anxiety research to encompass mood, affect, emotion, life events, social context and the like should improve matters considerably, there remains a need to reconsider what researchers are referring to when they focus on competitive anxiety and stress. Much confusion in the literature could be avoided if researchers relied upon the original and arguably best account of psychological stress provided by Selye and began to consider anxiety according to May as, 'the apprehension cued off by a threat to some value that the individual holds essential to his existence as a personality' (May, 1977: 205). Such a powerful and rich account of anxiety helps explain the existence of this phenomenon across a disparate set of situational domains. For example, it explains how the same individual may experience identical emotions before giving a presentation to their peers and in very different circumstances, before teeing off in front of friends at a social golf match. In these cases the affective sensations and cognitions may not be very similar and yet, from a phenomenological perspective, the individual may experience the feeling of disintegration, fear and desire. This anxiety during both experiences may last throughout the event or may dissipate as soon as activity is commenced. However, according to the existentialists, it is a normal and indeed unavoidable aspect of life. More controversially, as far as all other schools of psychology and sport psychology are concerned, this form of anxiety is considered healthy and should be sought out and *not* avoided!

An important and increasingly influential movement within sport and exercise psychology during the past two decades has forced sport psychologists and researchers to review their work in terms of its usefulness from an applied perspective. The growing professionalization of sport psychology and the introduction of certification and accreditation schemes for sport psychologists in North America, Australia and Britain continue to shape practice and research and even impact upon the content and structure of undergraduate and postgraduate programmes. In terms of stress and anxiety in sport, applied sport psychologists are increasingly involved in instructing athletes in meditative techniques, progressive muscular relaxation, visualization and other forms of MST. However, it has been suggested that clinically trained sport psychologists, especially those following the psychoanalytical tradition, have frequently employed depth techniques such as hypnosis and dream analysis in their work with athletes where more straightforward approaches, for example simple goal setting or counselling would have been more appropriate. In contrast, sport psychologists originally from a physical education background are likely, according to some, to possess too narrow a background in psychology and tend to rely excessively on packages and techniques that lack sufficient depth and have not been tailored to meet individual requirements.

This debate about approach in applied work has been taken up by Corlett (1996) who has argued that sport psychology must be aware of relying on what he calls, Sophist counselling, where athletes are taught MST techniques to make symptoms go away. Instead, he has passionately argued that sport psychologists will often need to provide much more than this and should be prepared to encourage the athlete to follow a process of self-examination leading ultimately to self-knowledge. Corlett has tried to distinguish between what he has referred to as Socratic counselling and Sophist approaches, by considering how each would deal with competitive anxiety. According to Corlett, a Sophist sport psychologist would focus exclusively on competitive anxiety as an interfering variable, the removal of which will lead to (cause) improved performance. He claims that in:

> Understanding anxiety as the product of high physiological arousal and negative thoughts, a Sophist might routinely, successfully, and exclusively teach athletes to manage it by somatic or cognitive strategies. The intent would be not to confront or understand anxiety but to eliminate its influence.
>
> (Corlett, 1996: 87)

However, whilst this approach may work for the motivated, well clarified, focused athlete who is more or less content with life, some problems cannot be solved meaningfully by MST alone. It is in such situations where the sport psychologist often needs to consider the broader social context and life experiences of the athlete. As Corlett puts it, 'sometimes the problem at its fundamental level is not the athlete alone, but the interactions of the athlete with coaches, parents and the sport itself' (Corlett, 1996: 90). This approach links closely to the existential account of anxiety and how it can be understood in applied sport psychology.

Investigating anxiety in sport – methodological issues

In his review of research developments and issues in competitive anxiety in sport, Jones (1995) highlighted the need to use different approaches in the study of anxiety. According to Jones, qualitative methodologies have been little used by researchers in the area; it is suggested this is unfortunate given that qualitative approaches may provide a more complete method for examining the social context within which competitive anxiety is experienced. Jones has gone further in suggesting that self-report measurements such as the CSAI-2 (Martens *et al.*, 1990) have largely failed to facilitate the precise measurement of anxiety. This situation, it is argued, is due to the difficulty of assessing a psychological state solely from the measurement of cognitive and somatic symptoms. Lane *et al.* (1999) have questioned the use of the CSAI-2 as a valid measure of competitive state anxiety. Their study involved 1213 subjects who completed the CSAI-2 one hour before competition. Confirmatory factor analysis revealed that the factor structure proposed by Martens *et al.* (1990) is flawed. In addition, this study revealed that there are difficulties within the cognitive anxiety scale around the word 'concerned'; athletes did not interpret this as worry or negative thoughts, but as a declaration about their motivation and willingness to meet a challenge.

Jones and other researchers (e.g. Swain and Jones, 1992) have identified a further weakness of current self-report anxiety measures, in that they cannot be used 'in vivo' to assess anxiety levels during competitive performance. This has led researchers (Terry, 1995) to suggest that new and shorter self-report measures need to be developed, and that greater use should be made of physiological and behavioural assessments during the sporting performance. However, it does appear doubtful that physiologically based measures will be able to do much more than record arousal levels. Earlier research in the area investigating physiological arousal in parachutists (Fenz and Epstein, 1967) and arousal, stress and motor performance (Oxendine, 1970; Neiss, 1988) was unable to clearly identify the exact aetiology of the symptoms and could not adequately overcome the fundamental conceptual problem of relying on objective arousal measures to assess the essentially subjective psychological state of anxiety.

That the major approach to the study of competitive sport anxiety during the past ten to fifteen years has been that of trait psychology, owes much to Martens' development of the SCAT (1977) and the CSAI-2 (Martens *et al.*, 1990). However, researchers (Gill, 1994; Jones *et al.*, 1996) have increasingly called for the inclusion of emotion and mood to be considered in work on both stress and anxiety in sport. This represents recognition as Fischer (1970) has argued that the study of anxiety cannot be advanced by the continued acceptance of a dualistic Cartesian metaphysics which separates meaning from affect.

Combined qualitative and quantitative methodologies according to Fischer (1970) and Caruso (1964), are able to build on the genuine and worthwhile findings of more traditional approaches, and accommodate much of the vigour and vitality of data that emerges from completely qualitative approaches. This integrated approach must not be simply defined as eclectic according to Assagioli (1993), but represents a new organic synthesis where unity and fidelity to both traditions are the goals. An integrated approach holds out great promise in the field of research if it can achieve a creative and meaningful reconciliation of two antithetical positions; on the one hand, the apparent duality of the self, and the real unity and uniqueness of the self on the other.

An important development in terms of providing a methodology that allows qualitative and quantitative data to be gathered simultaneously, involves the use of diaries. The diary has been recommended by psychotherapists such as Assagioli, in that it, 'gives a psychological film of the dynamic development of the patient's psychological state, of his mind stream' (Assagioli, 1993: 70). He suggests that the keeping of a diary provides a means of self-expression, and encourages the development of will, concentration and attention. Assagioli has also advocated that diaries can be used as an intervention technique in psychotherapy.

Within the mainstream, researchers interested in mood and emotional states have begun to utilize diary based methodologies in their work (Verbugge, 1980; Clark and Watson, 1988; Stone *et al.*, 1993). Diary approaches have recently been used by researchers investigating relationships between mood and exercise addiction (Sewell *et al.*, 1996) and the impact of exercise on mental states

(Clough *et al.*, 1996). These studies used four week daily mood diaries, which included analogue or bipolar scales and short, open-ended sections where subjects could provide more rich and in-depth qualitative data. According to Clough *et al.* (1996), such an approach allows the researcher to provide ecologically valid and in-depth results, which are nevertheless amenable to quantification and rigorous analysis. In combining the strengths of strictly qualitative and quantitative methodologies, the diary-based approach facilitates group analysis and investigation from an intra-individual perspective.

Future directions and new approaches

In conclusion, it appears that the reliance on the CSAI-2 has continued even where researchers cite the urgent need to employ a range of other methodologies and methods of data collection. Rather than following the suggestions made by Nesti and Sewell (1999), and Lane and Terry (1998) that mood should be considered alongside anxiety and performance, researchers have increasingly turned their attention to investigate the intensity and directional dimensions of competitive anxiety in sport. In addition, new research has emerged which focuses on the relationship between competitive anxiety in sport and a number of other psychological constructs, for example, self-presentation (Wilson and Eklund, 1998) and perfectionism (Hall *et al.*, 1998). Whilst this body of research can claim to represent a fresh change in direction, the issue of facilitating and debilitating test anxiety has been studied in the mainstream for over 40 years since the work of Alpert and Haber (1960). Whilst Jones *et al.* (1996) and others have continued to rely on the CSAI-2 in their work on debilitative and facilitative anxiety in sport, mainstream researchers such as Raffety *et al.* (1997: 894) have begun to utilize diaries to investigate anxiety and coping in academic test anxiety. Their work proceeds from a process orientated approach, which 'involved multiple assessments of anxiety or coping before or after (or both) an academic examination'. This approach allows a fine grained analysis of anxiety through longitudinal designs involving the completion of daily diaries. Although Raffety *et al.* have focused on facilitating and debilitating anxiety in their work, their results revealed that anxiety remained elevated after the exam for the high debilitating test anxiety group. From an existential approach to anxiety, this result is not very helpful in terms of understanding how subjects actually experienced these feelings of debilitative anxiety, although it does represent a step in the right direction. At least with the diary based approach it is possible to access some qualitative account (even if this is rather brief) to provide a more in-depth and personal description of the context within which the anxiety was experienced.

Recent research has utilized a diary based methodology to examine the experience of anxiety and mood in elite netball players and Super League senior rugby league referees (Nesti and Sewell, 1999) and with rugby league players (Nesti, 1999). These studies enabled both qualitative and quantitative data to be gathered longitudinally from 26 participants in elite level sport. This allowed for both idiographic and group based analysis of mood and anxiety scores. In addition, the inclusion of rich qualitative data provided within the daily diaries meant that the meanings that individuals attached to the experience of mood and anxiety could be more fully interrogated. Unlike in previous studies using diaries, the respondents were asked to provide qualitative material that would assist the researcher to examine the meaning each attached to their anxiety experiences. A number of interesting findings emerged from this work, which arguably would be difficult to identify with more traditional questionnaire-based approaches. For example, the daily diary data revealed that for most individuals anxiety did not rise in the predicted way prior to involvement in competitive sport, and that anxiety and other mood states were more influenced by important non-sport-related life events. The data suggested that anxiety could be better understood as being either a negative mood state associated with a real or perceived failure, or a more positive state associated with anticipation of a desired event. The former may be referred to as disappointment anxiety and may be more of a problem in sport than previously thought. It could be that negative anxiety after the match has been an important and largely overlooked area in the research to date and that its effect on future performance and motivation should be studied more closely. The latter could be labelled as anticipation anxiety, which describes that mood state where we anxiously look forward to a challenge which we relish. This idea is closely related to the concept of normal anxiety, which existential psychology has identified as being associated with growth and as such, not a negative mood state.

The diary based methodology revealed a number of important features that could enhance the ecological validity of sport anxiety research. The findings of the study with rugby league players (Nesti, 1999) has stressed the need to consider the social embeddedness of anxiety in sport, in particular in team situations. In addition, the diary methodology allowed for a process orientated approach where data can be collected during a period up to an event, and in the immediate aftermath and beyond. Raffety *et al.* (1997: 893) have also argued that longitudinal designs using daily diaries can 'minimize the problem of retrospective recall by making reporting periods more proximal to the experience'.

Critics of diaries have pointed out that adherence problems can result in poor completion rates. Bull and Shambrook (1998) have pointed out that self-motivation is the key to adherence in MST. It could be postulated that if athletes often struggle to complete MST despite being aware that such programmes are ultimately aimed at improving their sports performance, daily diaries may present an even less appealing commitment. In Nesti's study (1999), that the most detailed, complete and thorough daily diaries were provided by players who failed to achieve selection for one of the matches, or who performed well below their expectations, suggests that mood and anxiety diaries could be used by players to help them cope with unwelcome events. In addition, they may benefit from the experience of self-analysis and be able to help rekindle motivation, self-confidence and focus as a result of completing the brief written accounts in their diaries. However, although addressing adherence to MST

Gordon's (1990) comments may serve as a warning in expecting too much from diary methodologies in sport. In discussing work with national level Australian cricketers, Gordon warned that:

> The main problem I have is getting players to write anything down. Despite my efforts at devising user-friendly workbooks and explaining the benefits of written records only 40–50% of players seem willing to commit their thoughts to paper on this or any topic.
>
> (Gordon, 1990: 393)

Conclusion

In conclusion, despite some important drawbacks, the use of daily diaries may help investigators move closer towards a more complete existential analysis of a person's experience of anxiety in sport. In addition, this method connects well with the principles of phenomenology in that it allows the respondents to enter descriptions of the experience of anxiety in their own terms, rather than those provided by the psychologist.

In terms of a consideration of emotional volatility and mood liability which appeared to be an important factor in studies by Schimmack and Diener (1997), Nesti (1999) and Nesti and Sewell (1999) it appears that individuals who experience high levels of positive affect tend also to experience intense unpleasant affect. Diaries can be used to capture these fluctuations more easily than the repeated use of self-report inventories, and may begin to provide a more detailed and rich explanation of how and why this experience occurs. In discussing the need for studies to consider both the intensity and frequency of affect, Schimmack and Diener (1997) have pointed out that traditional one-shot approaches relying on a single inventory are unable to distinguish between two people, who although they experience similar levels of intensity, do so for different frequencies. For example, with one individual the experience of anxiety may be prolonged and remain at a given level for several days, compared to a different individual for whom anxiety, albeit at a similar intensity, is a more rarely experienced state. The diary based methodology used with the netball players, rugby league referees and players in Nesti's work included bipolar analogue scales which were easy and quick to complete. This data facilitated the identification of baseline levels for each variable, and enabled intra-individual comparisons to be made regarding intensity and frequency of mood states and anxiety.

Parkinson *et al.* (1996) have argued that a new methodology is required that allows for a detailed quantitative analysis of mood states, but will still be able to capture the richness, complexity and variability of mood. In terms of broadening the scope of studies in the area, Parkinson *et al.* have claimed that both the social and the temporal dimension need to be considered in studies into anxiety and mood, and that new methodologies and approaches are urgently required to meet these needs.

Problems remain despite the findings from studies such as Nesti (1999), which have begun to illustrate that a combined approach using a daily diary, a self-report sports specific inventory and match performance data can be used together to investigate mood, anxiety and performance in sport. It could be argued, that the major problem is the difficulty faced by researchers in attempting to combine nomothetic and ideographic data in a way which does not mean that the validity of each is severely weakened. Nevertheless, a diary approach had not been used previously to investigate anxiety in sport, and it may be that its use in the future will force researchers to consider anxiety and mood together, and to examine the social and temporal dimensions mentioned by Parkinson *et al.* (1996).

Further, the diary methodology may even encourage researchers to confront some of the serious limitations of the multidimensional approach to anxiety and end the suffocating over-reliance on the CSAI-2. Indeed, the concept of sport anxiety itself may even be subject to a closer and more phenomenological analysis, and attention could profitably be devoted to the search for subtle, in-depth and ultimately more ecologically valid accounts of this very real, yet elusive concept in sport.

Researchers (Lazarus, 2000) are moving towards greater recognition of the important role of the environment in the study of sport anxiety. Calls to place the sport anxiety experience within the social context of competitive sport seem to be along the right lines. An even more meaningful addition would be to begin to interpret sport anxiety from within the context of an individual's life. This approach has been considered within some of the final studies alluded to here, and the findings have gone some way to supporting the belief that anxiety must be studied whole and against the back cloth of an individual's life. Although not easy to achieve, such an approach may allow the researcher to differentiate more clearly between anxiety and excitement, and to consider the individual's psychological life from a holistic perspective involving a continuous stream of emotions and cognition, rather than as a series of discrete and unrelated mental events and their physical correlates.

Finally, in order to rescue research in sport and anxiety from the theoretical cul-de-sac it now seems to occupy, much greater attention should be devoted to considering older and much more complex accounts of anxiety. In practical terms, it may mean that researchers will need to redirect their focus away from the aridness of much North American sport psychology research largely based as it is on the tenets of behaviourism, neo-behaviourism and trait psychology, and turn towards more fruitful, rich and subtle European approaches to an understanding of anxiety. Fortunately, there are some signs that important questions are being asked in the area. In his review of the role of emotion in sport, Lazarus (2000) has pointed out that anxiety can facilitate performance in sport and that few key *contextual* factors have been explored in relation to the impact of anxiety on sports performance.

For sports anxiety research, the choice must be made. It is either more of the same, or a way forward that seeks to study anxiety rather than merely its symptoms, and which is prepared to consider anxiety as something all people experience which can nevertheless be associated with growth and success, or fear and failure. In order to pursue this there needs to be a reconceptualization of anxiety in sport based on existential psychology. This will encourage both researchers and applied practitioners to allow sports performers themselves to provide an account of anxiety, which unlike most of the research in the area until recently, is easily recognizable to those who actually take part in competitive sport!

Part II

Application of existential sport psychology

Professional practice issues and existential counselling in sport

5 Existential counselling in sport psychology

Engaging in the *encounter*

Introduction

Although most general introductory texts on psychology and sport psychology (e.g. Hill, 2001) consider that existential psychology is an approach within the broad area of humanistic psychology, this ignores the many important differences between the two. Spinelli (1989), for example, has pointed out that humanistic psychology and existential psychology study conscious experience, adopt a holistic perspective and stress that human beings are unique and possess free will. However, in contrast to humanistic approaches such as client centred counselling (Rogers, 1961), existential psychology focuses on both the positive and the destructive, negative and difficult aspects of life in equal measure. Whilst this is portrayed by existentialists as a more balanced and veracious account of human experience and reality, many psychologists in the English speaking world and especially in North America have recoiled from what they see as the deeply pessimistic tenor within existential psychology. In addition, existential psychologists are committed to minimizing the use of technique within both research settings and therapy.

Although, not discussing existential psychology approaches to counselling in sport, Corlett (1996) has argued that much of psychology, including sport psychology, is in danger of becoming synonymous with MST, resulting in an obsession with technique and formal assessment. He has claimed further, that following cognitive–behavioural approaches, sport psychologists often appear to rely solely on, 'technique based symptomatic relief' (Corlett, 1996: 88).

However, many psychologists utilize cognitive–behavioural techniques in their work (Welsh-Simpson, 1998; Nesti, 2002) alongside a broader existential focus. This is most usually aimed at providing some temporary relief from symptoms to facilitate the continuation of the more extensive existentially focused work with a person.

Finally, a major difference with all other approaches in counselling psychology and psychotherapy is that the aim is to assist the person to face normal anxiety constructively (Schneider and May, 1995). Existential psychology is concerned with helping people to accept the ultimate freedom and responsibility in their lives; to live authentically despite the experience of anxiety which will always accompany this decision. This view of anxiety as something that can be viewed favourably because it is often associated with human development and personal growth is diametrically opposed to the position adopted by most practitioners in sport psychology. Research (Maynard and Cotton, 1993) and accounts of practice suggest that most in sport psychology utilize stress management or anxiety control techniques to eliminate this undesirable emotion. This is very different to the existential view. For example, in elite level contexts, the sport psychologist would be concerned with helping the athlete to work creatively and courageously to accept and confront the anxiety associated with remaining at the top. An approach to counselling in sport, based on existential psychology, will be particularly useful at moments of transition, change and crisis in an athlete's life. This has been discussed in relation to career transition in elite sport (Lavallee *et al.*, 2000) and where an athlete is preparing for a major sports event (Nesti, 2002). However, it may be argued that this approach can guide work with an athlete in any circumstances where they are dealing with the broad category of challenging and anxiety producing life events that do not fall into the clinical realm, but which nevertheless represent serious concerns for the person.

Counselling process

The sport psychologist operating according to the ideals of existential psychology must constantly attempt to demonstrate the personal psychological qualities of presence, empathy and commitment. Before dealing with each of these key terms in more detail, it is important to highlight that this approach to counselling places considerable demands on the sport psychologist from an emotional and personal perspective. Existential psychology has emphasized that it is not counselling skills and techniques per se that are most important in effective work with a person, but rather, whether the psychologist can immerse themselves in the lived world (*Lebenswelt*) of their client. The sport psychologist must unreservedly give themselves over fully to the person with whom they are working. An existential encounter provides the environment to ensure that genuine empathy, authentic communication and a truly open meeting between two persons can take place. The encounter involves a rational working through of a key existential concern. This takes place between the psychologist and the client, and focuses on a process of clarification and on work towards making a choice to face up to the need to accept more personal responsibility to take decisions, in spite of the accompanying feelings of anxiety. In addition, the sport psychologist must assist this process by remaining with and alongside their client-athlete. Presence is essential as they struggle with what they need to do to convert their new awareness and greater self-knowledge into personally meaningful and concrete action in their lives. Given that the key existential concerns relate to death, freedom, isolation and meaninglessness, there is an expectation that the person will attempt to avoid the challenge to accept the action demanded as a result of their own clarification process during the encounter. This may result in the client attempting to deal with the anxiety of freedom by trying to evade the demands of choice and action. On other occasions, the person may temporarily withdraw from contact with the sport psychologist, or they may close up again and return to the original anxiety they were feeling before any sessions took place.

This process can be described as involving a cyclical pattern, where the client-athlete may regress to the earlier stage of avoidance and inaction to escape from the anxiety associated with choosing. At these moments, the personal qualities of empathy, authenticity and presence are most important to help the client to confront the anxiety accompanying the consideration of the key existential issues, and to work out a course of action for themselves and to act upon this. It is at this juncture between ideas and activity in the world, that the person must engage in what has been described as, 'a leap of faith'. This describes where a person must have the courage to act and follow a particular choice, even though the gap of personal freedom has not been fully bridged by the careful and thorough examination of the issue and what should be done to move it forward. According to existential psychologists such as Schneider and May (1995), the genuine empathy and authentic communication demonstrated time and again at these inevitable and uncomfortable moments within an encounter, is crucial to the success of this work. In addition, a number of existential psychologists (Spinelli, 1996; Nesti, 2002) and others (Fromm, 1994), have stressed that the personality of the counsellor is of central importance to the success of any existential encounter. This will be discussed in greater depth later in this chapter, however, it is important to highlight that it is not a demand that the psychologist possesses a specific personality type, such as introvert, extrovert or any other category assigned by the personality theorist. In fact, what the existentialists are claiming is that the psychologist must possess a '*personality*' because it is only then that a person may meet a person. This is because within an encounter, the relationship is considered the key to success, however defined. Spinelli (1996: 190) has argued that, although impossible to fully satisfy, the psychologist should, 'be with and for their clients'. The relationship in an existential encounter is not aiming at finding a 'cure' or leading the client to self-fulfilment. Instead, it is more appropriate to view it as something like the PhD supervisor–supervisee relationship in an academic setting, where although one has the responsibility to pose the difficult questions and offer guidance, both move forward together side-by-side.

The aim of existential psychotherapy is to assist the client to clarify, 'what is there, rather than what is lacking' (Bretherton and Ørner, 2003: 136). This is achieved by encouraging the client to focus on how they relate to the world, and on the possibilities and constraints they face in pursuing their goals. It has been expressed in an even more dramatic and powerful way by Buber. He has claimed that the challenge for the psychotherapist is to assist with, 'the regeneration of a stunted person centre' (1970: 178–179). This can only be achieved where the therapist is prepared to enter into a relationship with the other person. For an encounter to take place between two persons rather than two individuals, it is essential that the qualities of authenticity, presence and empathy are central to the process. Such a need places great demands on the therapist or sport psychologist and highlights the importance of the personality in this approach. Before considering the issue of personality in more detail, it is important to examine what each of the three aforementioned terms refer to.

Being authentic

Authenticity is demanded from both the client and the sport psychologist or therapist. On the client's side, this describes the need to recognize the reality of our lives in that on one side we experience particular givens of existence such as our mortality and genetic make-up. However, on the other side we have freedom to act and to choose a way of being. Authenticity consists of accepting that this is our 'lot' and that it is only by living in such a way so as not to reside at either the pole of complete freedom, or of external determination, that we can find our true *selves*. The authentic self is possibly better understood as an ongoing project, a relationship which loses authenticity and reality when it abandons the preparedness to remain open and fluid. *Inauthenticity* therefore, is that situation, where as Kierkegaard expressed it, *the individual in being their self is not themselves!* Another way of expressing this is that our lives can be described as unreal, or to use Sartre's term, *false*, when we have evaded our freedom to choose a course of action by handing ourselves over to fate. Fate refers to a belief that we have no control over what we do or think and that at a deeper level, freedom and the possibility of doing what we truly feel and wish for, is an illusion. According to Cohn (1997), we tend to live much of our lives in this inauthentic condition. Nevertheless, prolonged inauthenticity in our lives increases the chances of psychological disturbance and is a barrier to permanent psychological development and personal growth. It is the role of therapy to help the client to see and understand this and to assist them to confront inauthenticity in their lives.

From the therapist's perspective, authenticity is essential to ensure that a real relationship or encounter takes place between the parties. The claim to authenticity is also based on the requirement to consider both the positive experiences and the tragic and destructive elements of life. Indeed, Spinelli (1996) has emphasized that existential psychology differs from humanistic psychology by giving equal consideration to individual freedom and choice, and to the limitations, failures and at times misery of human existence. The existential approach lays claim to authenticity in that it accepts that people may choose and develop in either a good or bad direction and that they have some choice in this matter. As Spinelli (1989) and Welsh-Simpson (1998) have stated, this view has not generally been welcomed in traditionally Protestant Anglo-Saxon cultures, where the Humanistic message of the innate goodness of human beings and denial of guilt has found a particular resonance.

The psychologist is required to help the client to confront the anxiety associated with making choices and facing change. Authenticity in relation to this task means that the psychologist must not provide the client with an easy or comfortable escape from the feelings of anxiety that they are experiencing. This is because existential psychology in fact sees this angst or anxiety as being a good thing (albeit unpleasant), in that it expands in relation to the growth in authenticity of the client. In other words, the greater the number or magnitude of choices the person is prepared to consider, the greater their feelings of anxiety, but the more authentic they are becoming. This view of course is largely alien to most other approaches in psychology, where attention is often only or primarily focused, on the removal of symptoms and in providing the client with techniques to minimize any anxious experiencing in the future. In contrast, existential psychology takes a very different view in that as Kierkegaard (1844/1944) has argued in his book, the *Concept of Dread*, that the greater the self, the more authentic the person, the greater the anxiety! It should be recalled that the justification for this is that existential psychology, most especially that drawing on the formulations of its Christian founder Kierkegaard, claims that anxiety is both part of and a requirement for growth as a person. By facing up to rather than evading anxiety, the individual develops faith and courage to face their freedom and life. Therefore, the existential thera-pist must work to help the client to accept that their challenge is to face choices and to accept responsibility for their decisions and actions, despite the feelings of anxiety that always accompany this process.

However, this move towards authenticity does not mean that the existential psychologist can identify a particular choice for the client to pursue. The thera-peutic aim is at once more modest than this and yet more difficult to accom-plish, because the psychologist must resist the temptation to provide the solution or to suggest the best choice. The aim is to, 'aid persons in recognizing their resistances to, and attempts to control, the changes in their lives, rather than guide them in any direct manner towards novel ways of change' (Spinelli, 1996: 187). The meanings and choices that the client makes may be informed by anyone and anything in the lived world beyond their encounter with the existential psychologist. It is through this that it is possible for the psychologist to work with a client to expand awareness of the need to face up to their capa-city and obligation to make choices in life (i.e. accept their existential freedom), without going beyond the professional boundaries of their role. For example, the ultimate meaning of life can be provided for by belief in God or by subscribing to an atheistic perspective. The existential psychologist is not able to direct their client to these or any other configurations of meaning, however, they are required to aid the client to accept the need to find meaning and to make choices rather than to escape from this exciting yet painful essential.

A therapeutic attitude

Another vital ingredient in existential practice is that the sport psychologist must adopt what has been called a *therapeutic attitude*. This will provide a philosophy of practice and help guide the work within each encounter. The therapeutic attitude should not be understood as representing a body of theory that drives the programme of work with the client. It does not provide the psychologist with a ready-made list or guide of dos and don'ts in terms of how to conduct a session. Instead, it requires that the therapist view the client according to a number of critical anthropological themes. According to Moss (1989), these consist of an acceptance of mind–body unity, the recognition that we exist only in relation to others and that we are in a process of becoming. That is, we are future oriented. This philosophical armoury of the existential psychologist must be brought to life and impact on all of their work with the client and can be used to judge the success of the encounter. In addition, by continually reflecting on these themes before, during and after encounters with a client, it is possible to gain a deeper understanding of their struggles without limiting these to a specific set of desired outcomes or goals. Moss (1989) has pointed out it is by keeping this therapeutic attitude pre-eminent, that techniques and more narrow therapeutic modalities could be used sparingly by the existential psychologist. In this way, they will be able to employ techniques such as those based on cognitive behavioural approaches, without allowing these to interfere with the deep, existential encounter between two persons. Spinelli (1996) has argued that it is rare to see existential psychologists using psychometric tests and other diagnostic tests. However, there are some therapists who have apparently managed to combine psychoanalytical assessment methods within an existential framework (Schneider, 1995), although such individuals may be operating contrary to Freudian dogma by focusing on their 'client's capacity to verbalize their experiences directly, openly and bluntly' (Spinelli, 1996: 186).

Presence

The ideas of presence and commitment can be understood most clearly in comparison to the modus operandi of most other approaches in psychology. Psychoanalytic, behavioural and cognitive approaches, each in their own way, do not require the therapist to meet the client as an equal. Although humanistic psychology satisfies this dimension of client–psychologist parity and openness, the existential approach rejects any movement towards friendship between the two persons in an encounter. In this way, existential psychology is able to maintain the creative tension which is possible when there is 'distance' between people. However, that the psychologist must fully engage with the client and 'throw themselves' unreservedly into the encounter makes it possible for the therapeutic relationship to be dissolved temporarily.

It is within this interplay between the two poles of objectifying communication and of losing oneself in the other's *being* (of subjective communication), that the client and their psychologist can really be present to one another. This is difficult to achieve, especially on the part of the therapist because it can only take place where they listen to what the client has to say, rather than doing what most other approaches tend to do; assess, analyse and offer specific solutions. The use of descriptive questioning and the phenomenological rule of epoché or bracketing, represent two practical methods that assist the promotion of presence and the reality of communication within an encounter. The psychologist is required to work with the whole person and to stay focused on the *Lebenswelt*, which describes the 'world-as-lived' by the client. Focus is directed at what or how the person or the client is experiencing in their lives without resorting to abstract or theoretical terms to describe and explain this. This is a very important element in existential psychology research as well as in practice, in that through this it is hoped that the encounter is strengthened and protected. An added importance here is because for existential psychologists, 'the aim is to provide the client-athlete with an experience, not a cure or detached scientific analysis' (Nesti, 2002: 44).

Descriptive questioning really refers to the need to direct questions at what something means and how it is experienced by the person. The client must focus on the here and now (Spinelli, 1996) and reflect upon and clarify an issue or experience in their lives. This is a difficult task for both the client and the psychologist, however, it is considered to be vital to the success of the encounter. This is because, as has already been mentioned, the existential approach is not about providing clients with a detailed analysis of the causes of an issue and directing them to a remedial course of action. Therefore, the psychologist must avoid questions that seek to focus on the why and instead concentrate on dialogue aimed at the detailed description of an event or experience. It may frequently be a very emotionally exhausting and at times quite difficult experience for both the client and psychologist. For the psychologist, the strain is due to the need to demonstrate presence throughout the encounter and to 'resist the temptation to promote a particular solution for the client' which also 'ensures that the relationship, or encounter itself remains central to the process' (Nesti, 2002: 44). The client can be equally drained after an encounter. This is because they are being asked to confront and clarify, in rich detail, important personal events and experiences without being allowed to come to a quick answer themselves, or to hand over their responsibility to the psychologist to help them choose a particular course of action. This is an onerous yet essential element of the existential encounter and is clearly different to most approaches in humanistic psychology, where the accent is on finding new choices to assist personal growth.

Existential psychology is more concerned with the stages before the discussion of specific choices. Its focus is on helping the client to recognize that they have some control over their choices and that the acceptance of this existential fact and the act of making decisions and choosing will be accompanied by feelings of anxiety. It is the presence of the therapist within the encounters which facilitates this difficult and courageous self-examination by the client. By remaining fully present to the client in an encounter, it becomes possible for the division between the two individuals to temporarily disappear. They will then be able to move forward side-by-side as the client delves more completely and candidly into their lives.

In summary, the quality of presence involves, 'an attempt to remain present to the person with whom one is working' (Nesti, 2001: 204). In addition, it is important that the psychologist does not attempt to impose their own solutions and thoughts on the client. The aim is to assist the client to recover or uncover their freedom and to accept that this will usually involve feelings of discomfort. Beyond this very important, yet modest challenge, the task facing clients is to consider options and choices which will move them forward towards their desired goals and to personally accept some measure of responsibility for the final outcome.

Empathy

Existential and phenomenological therapists and researchers according to Polkinghorne (1989), use the process of bracketing (epoché) in an attempt to avoid imposing their own values and biases within an encounter. This is quite similar to the idea of unconditional positive self-regard, which is central to Rogerian psychotherapy. However, it differs in that bracketing is more aimed at preparing the therapist for an encounter than in helping the development of mutual respect and a non-judgemental relationship with the client. The idea is that by reflecting on their individual biases and personal history, the psychologist is able to develop greater self-knowledge of themselves. According to existential psychologists and many other key figures from the past such as Socrates, Plato, St Augustine and St Thomas Aquinas, the greater the self-knowledge the more prepared the *self is* to approach another person in humility and openness. The idea here is that the more transparent one's motives and thoughts are to oneself, the more one is able to accept that all human knowledge is incomplete and partial.

Empathy is essential within an existential encounter because it is through this that the psychologist is 'able to enter the clients' internal experiences of the world as far as is possible in order to reflect it back as accurately as they are able' (Spinelli, 1989: 130). Empathy can be enhanced through sound communication skills, such as active listening, clarity of oral expression, appropriate non-verbal behaviour and eye contact. However, according to the existential view genuine and deep empathy is developed through the personality of the psychologist. This stress on the person of the psychologist or psychotherapist and their centrality in the success of any encounter differs to all other approaches in psychology. The work of Buber (1958) has been used by many existential psychologists to explain how the person of the therapist or clinician is fundamental to the work with a client in a psychological setting.

According to Goldenberg and Isaacson (1996), the work of Buber has very considerable and important implications for the practice of psychotherapy. In particular, he has made an important contribution to the idea of personhood and the difference between individuals and persons. It is worth reiterating that existential psychologists have emphasized that the person of the therapist or sport psychologist, acting through their personality, is a most important element in the success of this approach. Berdyaev (1937) contends that a person can only grow, develop and learn in relation to *another* personality. It is the unique features of personality which allow the psychologist and their client to meet in an authentic encounter involving a total and unconditional level of communication. This is because of the holistic structure of personality in that, 'personality is my whole thinking, my whole willing, my whole feeling, my whole creative activity' (Berdyaev, 1937: 113). This description makes it easier to understand why personality and personhood is highlighted in existential psychology because it is associated with a spontaneous and full self-giving.

Buber has referred to this in terms of the I–Thou relationship. He has argued that, 'all genuine and authentic relationships are dialectical in that they progress in ever ascending spirals involving movement from what he calls the I–it mode of being to the I–Thou' (Nesti, 2001: 208). I–it refers to those occasions where the relationship between two persons is centred on use; that is what one can get from the other. In strict terms, this communication is between individuals and not persons as such, because the relationship is aimed at something *beyond*, which in turn reduces this relationship to something which is functional and utilitarian. When approaching another individual in the I–it mode we maintain our distance and as Berdyaev has pointed out, we treat them more like a thing or an object and not as a person. Of course, this type of relationship and level of communication can be successful in 'getting things' and has its legitimate place within our lives. For example, when we approach another for a particular service, in commerce or to access information, the I–it stance is congruent with what we are attempting to achieve. When I want to buy a new television, I want information on its performance relative to others, cost and other technical details. I am not looking for, and indeed might be intimidated and distracted by an I–Thou encounter in this situation.

In contrast, the client who comes to work with the psychotherapist or sport psychologist expects much more than an impersonal encounter. They hope for and according to existential psychology, need to experience, a situation where they are approached as a person and a personality by another personality where the relationship itself is the central and dominant feature. This describes the I–Thou relationship. In this mode of being, an unreserved, full and authentic encounter can take place. It should be remembered that for existential psychologists, the encounter itself is central to the 'success' of this approach and therefore, everything must be oriented towards this, rather than at specific outcomes or future actions. Personality facilitates this because it is not a thing or a means to an end. Instead, personality is more accurately to be conceived of as an end in itself, something which is free and may be better described as a spiritual category rather than a psychological concept.

Within sport psychology, the importance of the personality in the consulting process has received attention from Ravizza and Fazio (2002). In discussing their extensive experience of applied work in sports settings, Ravizza and Fazio (2002: 114) have stressed that, 'who they are has been a large part of their successful consulting relationships'. They have highlighted that personal qualities such as humour, integrity, trust and respect can be developed through education, self-reflection and experience. Whilst this appears to be closely related to the existential view of the importance of personality in the therapeutic process, educational project or consulting experience, there are some important differences. The greatest of these is that according to the existential perspective since the personality is what Berdyaev has called a unified and integrated whole, it cannot be improved and developed through an approach that is not holistic. This rejects the idea that personality can somehow be divided into a hierarchical set of categories and qualities and each nourished accordingly. Nevertheless, it is interesting to note that existential psychology and the work of Ravizza (2002a) in sport, argue that the person of the sport psychologist or counsellor is central to the encounter, or consultation process with a client or athlete. A further helpful contribution to the issue of personality development and growth has been provided by Spinelli (1996). He has suggested that alongside extensive, broad theoretical knowledge and applied experience, the existential psychologist must possess maturity, life experience and a high degree of self-knowledge. In terms of what constitutes the essential personal qualities, Spinelli contends that the existential-phenomenological counselling psychologist must be able to engage in:

> critical self-reflection, wide-ranging engagement with various cultures, environments and work-related situations, an ability to express and acknowledge the humour, tragedy and absurdity of living, and an ongoing curiosity about, and tolerance for the different ways people opt to 'be-in-the-world'.
>
> (Spinelli, 1996: 187)

One of the clearest differences between the existential view and others that are based more on cognitive and humanistic approaches is in relation to the issue of presence. It will be remembered that presence is something that must be demonstrated by the existential therapist or sport psychologist. In brief, this quality can be summed up as the open, unguarded self-giving of one person to another. At a deeper level, it describes where there is a complete absorption and total focus in another person *as an end in themselves*. This is what Buber (1958) refers to as a *Thou*. To facilitate this truly personal mode of communication requires much more than the use of appropriate listening skills, attentional focus and a sincere effort to be there for someone. The existentialists accuse other approaches in psychology of conveying the lie that the 'technical' skills of the expert listener can be learnt and acquired, and that these will facilitate the development of presence. In rejecting this conception outright, Marcel (1948) claims that presence depends on what he calls spiritual availability (*disponibilité*). This is best understood by considering that it belongs to those persons who listen not with their minds alone but with their hearts, minds and whole being. He offers that this presence can often literally be felt and 'reveals itself unmistakingly in a look, a smile, an intonation' (Roberts, 1957: 292).

There is much more demanded here than the following of a pattern of appropriate behaviours and a desire to be available and to offer help. Presence can be experienced across time and space. This powerful, in some ways mysterious quality also demands a response on the part of the person receiving it. When it is present it can be discerned even where the person is far from us. In contrast, mere physical proximity is not a guarantee of its existence, as can be seen where someone is in a room alone with another individual and yet despite this, there can be a sense of alienation and detachment. Again, the quality of presence has more in common with listening rather than hearing, although the existentialists would emphasize that the listening will involve more than either a cognitive or an emotional reaction, or both of these combined. Instead, it is better described as a total unreserved emptying of myself into the other person; a listening with my whole being prior to any division into separateness.

Finally, existential psychology insists that interpersonal parity exists between the client and the psychologist. However, this does not mean that there is a completely equal relationship, but more one where each of the parties is considered equal in human terms. In other words, they are able to meet as two persons but in a contextual setting where one has approached the other for some kind of help. Buber (1958) has pointed out that absolute parity on all things is not possible or desirable in the encounter for two reasons. The first is because the client has come to the therapist because they possess a level of knowledge, skills and professional expertise. This functional element cannot be removed or overcome, although it can be minimized. However, the second reason is both more positive and controversial, at least as far as humanistic psychology is concerned. Buber has pointed out that the creative tension that exists between client and therapist is essential to learning.

Spontaneity

Spontaneity is an important element within the existential encounter. Fromm (1994) has argued that the capacity to display spontaneous behaviour is related to psychological health. According to Fromm, we can only think and act in a spontaneous way when we are able to approach the situation or another person without the distraction of our own self-consciousness. In echoing Bubers I–Thou idea, it is only when we are prepared to approach the other as a Thou that spontaneity is possible. Spontaneity is important because it is when we reveal our true selves in the most transparent way possible. The most complete encounters between the client and the psychologist contain dialogue infused with spontaneity of words and thoughts. When we speak in a spontaneous way we reveal our authentic selves and authenticity is the *sine qua non* of existential psychology practice. However, the psychologist must be aware of the danger of allowing spontaneous conversation to degenerate into nothing more than a discussion around feelings, or about trivial matters unrelated and distant to the main concerns. This is of course difficult to achieve since it requires that the psychologist throw themselves into spontaneous dialogue whilst priming themselves to be capable of intervening to re-direct and guide the encounter when necessary. This is in some ways analogous to play behaviour and performing in competitive sport, in that whilst playing we are deeply engaged in the task. However, this does not mean that we are not able to be aware of the time, score or pattern and tempo of the game, and that we can adjust, reflect on or re-start the matter simultaneously.

Finally, Fromm (1942) has suggested that we are often most proud and excited by our spontaneous acts and that this is because we have experienced the satisfaction from doing or saying something of our very own. The recording of such dialogue by the therapist and its use in later sessions can be a very powerful way of encouraging the client to understand the benefits of authenticity. The continued presence and genuine empathy of the psychologist is the most important factor in helping the client to reside at the pole of spontaneity time and time again within an encounter.

Confronting anxiety in sport performance

Case study

The following account describes a series of encounters with a sports performer involving an existential psychology approach. This case study describes an example of a failure to face up to normal anxiety over a period of almost six years. These case notes relate to the reflection of the sport psychologist during a specific phase of work with the sports performer.

Having had six years of apparent success and achievement in her sport, the performer approached the sport psychologist for assistance after a particularly bad competitive performance. It became clear that there had been a repeated failure to confront normal anxiety and this had eventually become too much. Although not at the neurotic level, this anxiety was preventing the performer from making decisions and choices in her career. This was uncovered by a combination of existential analysis of her case history and the reaction to two MST techniques. The athlete described how she was completely unable to use imagery or positive self-talk (as prescribed for her earlier by another sport psychologist) because of the 'sheer terror' (her words) that overcame her as she prepared to initiate the sport task. She described how she tried to 'manage' the situation by trying to avoid responsibility to face up to this. But during matches and when called to perform her role, the 'thing' just appeared from nowhere, blotting out everything except a feeling of terror and being out of control. It seemed to come without warning and to destroy everything in its path. At moments like this she felt totally lost and relied on luck to get through the task. Each time she performed the task she felt that it could be her last! Her performances were declining rapidly.

She had used strategies over the years to try to overcome this, such as becoming recognized as 'the big character' of the team with a high profile and resilient personality. However, throughout this, she was aware that the anxiety was gnawing away and growing. She realised that she had been living inauthentically and that she now needed to draw closer to her real (authentic) self. This would mean that she had to begin to struggle with accepting a new and lower identity for herself and to start at the beginning again (whilst knowing that no one understands the pain and discomfort that she is facing). The gap had become too big between who she really was, and the high profile and responsibility of being a top performer and senior player. The bridge between the one identity and the other had sagged and almost broken! She was aware that she was right on the boundary line between normal anxiety and clinical neurotic anxiety – she was able to get by unaided in the rest of life beyond sport, but it was not a pretty sight!

After six encounters the sports performer had clarified her existential situation and had started to confront the need to return to authenticity. At this point she began to understand that her choices were to leave the sport, or to return to her self and face the normal anxiety again and again with courage and faith – aware that all of this would be very painful but was unavoidable to experience the full joys of her sports performance again. Only existential guilt at having avoided this for so long could prevent her from now moving on.

The anxiety here is related to May's idea of a threat to a value that the person holds as central to their existence. This value is based on a conglomeration of the views of peers, media, family, coaches and her own perception of herself as a top sports performer. She described that, 'she had been found out' and that her achievements in the sport were far beyond the perception she had of herself and the reality of her self.

Training supervision in sport psychology

Case study

This case study highlights the different demands associated with adopting an existential psychology approach towards the supervised experience process in sport psychology. There are a number of important differences between how a psychologist acting in a supervisory role with a trainee would proceed within an existential psychology approach, in comparison to a more humanistic psychology oriented outlook. The most important of these centre on the issue of anxiety, and its relationship to both learning and personal growth. In addition, the use of the encounter rather than a less emotionally laden and non-confrontational mode of working, as seen for example in most humanistic approaches, sets existential psychology based supervision apart. This way of working places particular demands on the supervising sport psychologist and the supervisee. It requires that the supervisor in the relationship constantly strives to attend to the key elements of authenticity, presence and empathy whilst maintaining a focus on the lived experience of the supervisee.

The supervisee was in the final phase of his training to become an accredited sport and exercise psychologist. His work role encompassed providing sport psychology support to a small number of elite level athletes and professional sports teams. All of the work with the teams was delivered by the trainee sport psychologist on a contractual basis. The support service details, in terms of hours and outline agreement on what would be offered by the sport psychologist, had been identified for a 12-month period. This contract had been agreed between the professional clubs and the sport psychologist's employer, and represented the third year of work undertaken by the sport psychologist with each of the teams.

The supervisor initially scheduled a series of meetings with the supervisee to ensure that frequent and regular meetings could take place between them. However, because of the volatile and highly unpredictable environments in which the professional sports teams were operating, it was agreed that a more flexible approach to the scheduling of meetings would be necessary. Further to this, close contact was assisted by maintaining email and telephone links during, and after the normal working day.

Whilst a significant amount of work between the supervisor and the supervisee focused on reviewing achievements and work programme goals, a far greater period of time was devoted to discussion around individual cases and the experiences of the supervisee. Increasingly, this latter element began to dominate meetings and the more informal contact between the sport psychologists. The supervisee began to reflect more systematically on his own skills and qualities as a sport psychologist, and began to consider deeper questions around how and, in what way could he be effective in his role at the clubs and in his dealings with other individual athletes. Within the face-to-face meetings in particular, the supervisor supported the supervisee in his efforts to explore questions around ethical dilemmas, dealing with personally challenging situations, and understanding his own and others' expectations of his role. This focus on increasing self-awareness and self-knowledge meant that, not infrequently, encounters between the supervisor and the supervisee were wrought with emotional involvement. According to existential psychology, the experience of strong emotional involvement in general, and feelings of anxiety in particular during an encounter are often signs that something of real and personal importance is actually being discussed between the parties.

The phenomenological interview was used within encounters between the supervisee and supervisor. This involves attending to questions surrounding what something is and how it was experienced. The aim is to assist the supervisee to focus on a rich description of an issue or event and to avoid any analysis of what these experiences may mean. For example, the supervisee during one encounter lasting 80 minutes described the experience of feeling powerless and ineffective when major media and financial influences combined to undermine his planned psychological support programme during a key phase in the season of a high profile professional sports club. The supervisor encouraged the supervisee to describe what he was experiencing during this uncomfortable and challenging period, and to use everyday language (i.e. not technical terms or psychological labels) to construct an in-depth account. In order to achieve this, the supervisor must guide the supervisee away from any consideration of possible explanations or analysis of the events and experiences. In simple terms this means that, the supervisor should refrain from questions around 'why' or 'how' and more properly concentrate on questions of 'what'. In this example, the supervisee described that he was feeling unsure about his role and effectiveness during this difficult and uncertain period for the club. He described in considerable detail that he had begun to think about his identity as a sport psychologist, and what he thought he had been able to offer the professional players, coaching staff and the club as a whole in terms of psychological support. This involved him in an increasing level of analysis of who he was and what he thought he did in his role as sport psychologist. This progressed away from a consideration of the current period, to reflection on what had been happening throughout the previous seven months of the season and what was about to take place in the remaining four weeks. This in turn, led back towards a more detailed account of the current experience in light of what had gone before and what was expected to occur in the near future. The supervisee began to describe his role as a sport psychologist in professional high profile sport, as being something closely connected to his broader personal identity. He began to describe how this experience of feeling confused about what he should do in situations where his plans were overtaken by other events beyond his control, was something that he experienced in other personal and professional relationships. This was something that he tried to counter by throwing himself into a range of tasks and activities. However, during the encounter he began to describe this pattern of busying himself as something which did not really make him feel effective, content or composed. In fact, it was at these times that he was most aware that what he was doing to address the challenge was actually making him feel even less confident and secure in his role. Again, examples of this type of behaviour were identified by the supervisee in other areas of his life and discussion of these was encouraged by the supervisor, despite this being a difficult and emotionally charged experience for both parties. During this intense moment within the encounter, the supervisor had to take great care to prevent a natural desire to identify possible solutions from interfering with the rich experiential account. However, with the existential approach, the supervisor is required to guide and direct the supervisee away from a more problem solving analysis, and back to a focus on describing the issue of concern. This requires that whilst the supervisor must continue to display the qualities of empathy and presence, they must nevertheless not allow the encounter to be diluted by any prolonged or sustained attempts by the supervisee to either move on to a consideration of less existentially significant concerns, or to suggest a way to resolve the issue. The aim is not to end the meeting with a list of action points, but to emerge after an encounter between two persons with a fuller understanding of a particular experience and to have developed a greater level of self-knowledge.

The existential encounter provides the supervisee with a relationship with someone who can empathize with them. This is considered to be a key ontological principle of existential psychology. It is assumed that all persons possess a need for a mentor, a guide or a teacher, with whom it is possible to experience genuine and deep empathy. This is particularly important for those persons who are isolated or operating in new and personally challenging environments. The supervisee was experiencing these elements in his role as sport psychologist to the professional sports teams. He was often faced with unfamiliar tasks and new demands, and often lacked an experience of similar situations to draw upon. The importance of having someone who could empathize with the supervisee and discuss their own related experiences in providing sport psychology support is highlighted as a cornerstone of the existential psychology approach to a supervision process. This clearly suggests that a prerequisite for good and effect-ive supervision is that the supervisor must possess an in-depth and broad range of practical experience in providing sport psychology support.

A further unusual feature of this approach is that it is accepted that it may be important to provide support and maintain links between the supervisor and supervisee outside of the normal working day. In this case, the supervisee was encouraged to contact the supervising sport psychologist at anytime outside of normal sleeping hours where the issue was considered to be of key existential significance. For example, within elite level professional sport, considerable changes can take place in team personnel over the course of a season. Transfers between clubs and the signing of new players can have a major impact on the success of a club, and often generates huge media interest and speculation. The managers and coaching staff are faced with new challenges in this situation, and these are often most pronounced where the incoming players are high profile and used to achieving success. The sport psychologist may be called upon to help the new players integrate into the team setting, and assist them as they accept new roles and tactics. Where players are from another country with very different cultural contexts, the demands on the new players can be extensive. The supervisee contacted the supervisor several times across a three-week period to discuss his role in supporting the newly acquired players. Contact took place in face-to-face meetings and by telephone; these sessions were not planned in advance and frequently occurred outside of the normal working day because this was often the only time that the supervisee could identify as being suitable to use for in-depth reflection on the work that he was doing with the new players. The supervisor agreed to make himself available to the supervisee in this way in order that he could provide support during this difficult yet excit-ing phase, and to ensure that there was an opportunity to focus on what the sport psychologist was experiencing and feeling during what for him was a new situation. The supervisor's role during these encounters was to provide empathy and presence, and to encourage the supervisee to face up to the doubt and anxiety, which confronted him as he made choices and decisions in relation to helping the new players and the club progress. It is important to recognize that the supervisor is primarily interested in standing alongside the supervisee as he wrestles with reflection on the action he has taken and what option he may choose next. This can only be achieved where the supervisor throws himself fully into the encounter, and devotes his full and intense concentration to what is being discussed. It can make the experience quite emotionally demanding for the supervisor but is considered absolutely essential to ensure that empathy and presence are truly felt by the supervisee during the encounter. Authenticity in the depth of communication is a vital ingredient in assisting the supervisee to adopt an open and self-critical perspective in discussing their work and role. This is most important where the material being discussed is new to them or has ethical and moral dilemmas attached to it.

However, whilst the supervisee is helped to think about their choices and decisions, this does not mean that they are in control of the encounter. The supervisor has to ensure that the discussion avoids losing depth and focus, and make sure that the supervisee is guided towards, in some way, a consideration of the existential significance for them of what they have been attempting to do. For example, the task of working with new players was understood in a way that drew on his own previous experiences of being in a new situation. The supervisee discussed how he had been unable to deal effectively with the new players because he had assumed that with their international reputations and breadth of experience in the sport at the highest level, they would easily be able to settle into their new club and the different culture with little support. That this had not occurred led the supervisee to consider that what these players were experiencing was similar to the feelings, perceptions and anxieties that other players had mentioned to him when they faced a new challenge. This in turn led to a consideration of what he had felt like in new work settings, after promotion or where his own role had changed rapidly. By considering the feelings and events around these situations he was able to identify that it was the small things, like being introduced to new colleagues and attention being directed at helping his family settle in, that helped confidence the most. These small matters were of even greater importance to the more experienced players, as it was expected that this type of support was only needed for those starting out in their careers. The supervisor guided the supervisee to consider what this new learning meant in terms of his own understanding of the role of a sport psychologist working in elite level sport and beyond, and to identify how he might act upon this in the future.

The role of the supervisor is always to help the supervisee to develop courage to move ahead in spite of feelings of anxiety and even despair. The aim of each encounter is to assist the person to face up to their responsibility, to make choices and to reflect that this is no guarantee that what they choose will always be the right course of action. Nevertheless, the acceptance that a person has some say in the matter of what takes place in their lives and that they must strive to face up to the idea of accepting personal responsibility for their actions, is seen as central to the development and growth of an individual. This is facilitated by the supervisor during the encounter with the supervisee, and through use of follow up meetings and reports. These written reports allow the parties to look again at the events and issues that they have discussed, and to reflect on whether there are other elements missing from the description of an issue or situation. In addition to this, the supervisor may extend their report and case notes to include reference to further reading alongside their own insights into how the supervisee's experience relates to key existential psychology themes such as values, courage, creativity, choice and responsibility. The aim is to help the supervisee to expand their self-awareness and self-knowledge in recognition that it is through this, rather than through the application of particular techniques or the discussion of work programmes, that they will be more likely to affect their clients in a constructive way.

6   Professional team sport

Operating within an existential framework

Introduction

The coach, sports scientist or sport psychologist operating within team sports face particular challenges that are different to those operating in individual sports. In addition, at the highest levels of team sports there are a range of contextual factors that impact on the feelings of autonomy and control of the coach or sport psychologist. For example, the sport psychologist working with elite professional sports teams is often attempting to provide a service in a very volatile and publicly sensitized environment, where each day brings significantly differing problems to be addressed and obstacles to be overcome. Media intrusion, injuries, transfer requests, interference from the club owners and job uncertainty are just some of the elements that must be faced by the sport psychologist in these settings. It can be argued that to survive and indeed thrive in such an arduous climate, sport psychologists will need to possess resilience, commitment and the personal qualities of presence, authenticity and empathy. Time management, and organizational and communication skills are also important tools for the sport psychologist in this demanding milieu. Existential psychology claims that the crucial factor in the psychologist's armoury is their personality, and it is through the expression of this that they will be able to offer a truly psychological input for the benefit of the other staff and players within the team sports organization. The existential perspective would accept that whilst there may be much benefit to the team or sports club (franchise) through improving their communication and management processes, the most important and authentically psychological work can only be achieved at a personal level between two individuals. This may be more possible to facilitate in an individual sports situation where one-to-one work is easier to pursue. However, the existential view would be that this level of contact is needed and is arguably even more essential where the person is an integral part of a larger group, team or organization. In dealing with this requirement to provide for the personal and the individual within the team environment, the existential psychologist will need to continually reflect critically on their own practice, beliefs and values. Through this difficult and courageous process of self-examination, the existential psychologist will develop greater self-knowledge. This, and not the more peripheral task of self-awareness, is key, as it is about the growth and development of the deepest core of being. This is the base where our authentic self is located; this core must be constantly confronted and fed for its growth. The result of this, which is always an unfinished task, is that the existential psychologist will develop a firm core self that nevertheless (apparently paradoxically) will increase in flexibility. This can be seen at one level in terms of those personalities with a high degree of self-knowledge and a well-clarified core, who possess values they have struggled to make their own. Such persons, irrespective of vocation or professional occupation, are able to truly communicate with other people from very different situations. This important quality is essential for genuine empathy to exist between two individuals and is central to the existential encounter.

The case study below details the clarification process and critical analysis engaged in by a sport psychologist working in elite level professional sport. In this example, the material presented is based on an in-depth phenomenologically framed interview with the sport psychologist. An existential psychology interpretation is provided throughout the discussion of the case. This highlights the key existential themes that are being considered, and offers an interpretation of the activities of the sport psychologist from an existential psychology perspective.

Case study

The sport psychologist had been working full-time with a professional sports organization for a number of years. The interview took place towards the end of the playing season and focused on addressing the phenomenological accounts of what had been experienced over the season and how these had felt.

The sport psychologist (SP) began by considering what he felt like at this particular moment. The existential psychologist (EP) asked the SP to focus on what he was experiencing right now. The SP described that he was feeling as though he had been given a respite from the crushing momentum and tension of the final days of the season. He had a dull feeling as though he was a character in an unreal story in a book. The main sensation was of being a passive bystander who was no longer able to feel strongly about the outcome, despite being calmly aware that the final outcome was extremely important to all at the club, including his own future. He talked about how he could recognize this feeling as being different to the studied, detached and professional aura that he had been able to cultivate across the year as a whole. This 'controlled' and impassive style reflected the belief that the SP had 'done his job well' and that the players and other staff had been prepared thoroughly for each challenge. The authenticity of this manner and demeanour now provided a clear point of difference with his current feelings and thoughts. In confronting this, the SP attempted to clarify what this meant for him. This led to a discussion around learning and how he had learnt more about himself and key others such as the team managers, senior coaching and technical staff during the past season. The last two months had provided a hugely volatile and emotionally charged learning environment that only now was he really aware of. This intense experience had led him to reflect on what he had truly learnt, and to acknowledge that this traumatic phase had helped him to assess his career to date and what he hoped for in the future. The EP asked the SP to consider what it felt like to talk about his future during this very difficult stage for his club at the season's climax. The SP declared that he felt excited about this but not emotionally speaking at this moment. This was explained by the SP as being something which he felt in greater control of now, than at any time in the last few years in his working life and that he was now more content to get to the next challenge more slowly. This sense of progressing and developing at a more balanced and equitable pace towards his vocational goals had increasingly extended to the rest of his life. The SP described his experience at the team as being a sacrifice that was often painful and difficult at times. However, it was an experience that was accepted and even welcomed because it was something he had chosen. He used the term 'accountability' to explain how he had, 'put this responsibility upon himself rather than having it thrust upon him by others'. Therefore, he had always felt personally involved and committed to his current work, and his future career and broader life goals, despite many difficult and tense periods.

Existential psychology interpretation

An important existential issue that emerged clearly during this stage of the encounter was that the SP was able to discuss the differences between real learning and being able to remember facts. This has been cogently expressed by Colaizzi (1978) in terms of the distinction between information acquisition and *genuine learning*. According to the existential view, material that is not related to our existence, which therefore is impersonal in the strictest sense, is more accurately described as information acquisition. This is very different to genuine learning, which although often difficult or hard to achieve, is never forgotten because it is about our self rather than a series of existentially irrelevant structures. This means of course, that following this view, we do not often genuinely learn in our lives. The SP seemed to be claiming that especially during the very challenging final phase of the playing season he had experienced authentic learning. His account of what had been learnt was again consistent with Colaizzi's existential psychology account, in that it was not about this or that fact, but about something personally meaningful and more related to self-knowledge than about an understanding of new strategies and cognitive skills. In speaking about the area of psychology devoted to the study of learning, Colaizzi (1978: 133) has challenged the prevailing orthodoxy that tries to convince us 'that the ever increasing accumulation of factual data and information, especially that generated by technologico-explanatory approaches, is the mark of education, wisdom and learning'. In addition, he contends that genuine learning is never boring given our full involvement in it, although it is often very demanding and difficult. It requires our full selves to be present; genuine learning insists that the whole person must be attuned to the task. This is very different from the more easily forgotten type of learning that only takes place at a purely cognitive or emotional level.

The SP was unsure at this stage exactly what he had learned; had he been required to list the specific components of his learning experience he would have been unable to perform this task. He was acutely aware that through the anxiety and discomfort of the past two months in particular, he had to 'do his job' as team psychologist and that he had only been able to do this in very perilous circumstances, by taking time to reflect on what he stood for. This meant that as the encounter dialogue makes clear, he reaffirmed to himself that he had chosen his current path and that he now understood that acting on his existential freedom to choose would always be accompanied by both sacrifice and joy. The SP also began to recognize that the learning experience during the season was very valuable in relation to making choices about the next stage of his vocation as a sport psychologist. Again, the existential encounter is less interested in an analysis of which particular courses of action that the person should pursue next. Instead, the focus is aimed at encouraging the client (the SP in this case) to really grasp that they have some control over what they will do in the future, and to accept the anxiety and excitement associated with this 'thought' without trying to avoid this by prematurely selecting a specific choice. Such patience and fortitude in relation to choices could be described as mental toughness. It involves that authentic and personally meaningful choice is substantially within a person's orbit should they be courageous enough to face up to this. According to existential psychology, that most people attempt to ignore this call to personal freedom in their vocations, careers and broader lives by either choosing quickly without deep self-reflection or by conforming to the views of others, reveals that most would rather escape from this part of our being. Fromm (1942) has called this fear of freedom the source of many of our social and individual ills. The SP recognized that when the environment and what Berdyaev (1937) calls the *world of necessity* threatens to take over control of a person, they must return to their selves and accept their capacity to say a 'yes' or a 'no' to events and ideas. In other words, the SP had acknowledged that he was required to make decisions and judgements in his work and in relation to broader life, and not to do this would involve him abdicating the responsibility to choose. This choosing of course is accompanied by a recognition that the act of choosing does not guarantee that the choice will be the best or most appropriate. However, by facing up to the responsibility that freedom and choosing does not always lead to the desired outcome is to live in and through what has been referred to as destiny. Destiny is a term used to describe the life lived in hope; where the person participates in their future in spite of the knowledge that it is never fully in their control. This can be contrasted with relying on luck or fate where the individual has adopted an air of resignation and has abandoned the idea that they can influence the unfolding of their lives. Existential psychology according to Clark (1973) is able to provide a view which is neither overly pessimistic nor excessively optimistic with regard to our freedom. It chides humanistic psychology for a one-sided approach, which appears to claim that a full personal freedom is possible (and desirable). On the other side, the determinist paradigms of psychoanalysis and behaviourism are denounced for their pessimistic refusal to grant human beings any agency at all!

Case study

The SP described how his experiences in the job provided for what he referred to as, 'global learning'. He explained that this related to a recognition that it was his passionate interest in the tasks he did, which provided the opportunity to satisfy his desire for learning. This learning was something that he felt was more 'real' than even the outcomes of the specific tasks and situations he was involved in. The SP claimed that through giving himself fully to the success of each scenario, he was able to feel and act creatively even where employed in more structured and formal activities like a team meeting. Increasingly, he had found himself reflecting on what he had done and the achievements that resulted when he had completed some work. This had led to quite depressing and uncomfortable periods of self-reflection and appraisal. However, the SP explained that whilst he accepted that his commitment to such intense, deep self-analysis and personal reflection brought increased intrinsic motivation and excitement, it often resulted in bouts of self-doubt and anxiety. The SP talked about his evolution from being someone who always needed to know what made something successful to being prepared, more frequently, to pass over questions of why and how. He suggested that an important lesson, especially during the fraught and difficult final two months of the season, was that he had begun to accept that what he had learnt and how to put this into practice on other occasions rarely emerged until well after the event. This was richly expressed as being like waiting for something very important to happen but which cannot be forced in terms of timing or even its eventual appearance. To an individual with a very high work ethic operating in a high profile, pressured and rapidly changing environment, this lesson was and remained a difficult one to fully accept.

In terms of practical assistance in managing this tension, the SP explained that the concept of a role model had become an important idea for him. He talked about how he had increasingly seen that a very important part of his job as a sport psychologist was to provide a role model for others and crucially for himself! On a day-to-day basis, this demanded that he constantly tried to present his values, standards and expectations through his own behaviour and ideas to other staff and players at the club. These standards and values were reinforced by his experiences at other organizations and through his work with high achieving performers in a range of domains. Where he failed to demonstrate these in his role as SP there was a feeling of having let himself down. This was often followed by deep reflection, and a recommitment to remain true to these values and standards. The SP also talked about the emotionally draining experience of working in an environment where standards and individual's commitment to personal excellence often fell short of the mark. The frustrations emanating from these particular experiences have been used by the SP to assess his own career and personal needs. He discussed how he had begun to see more clearly that to be effective now meant that he needed to know what he wanted to experience in the future. Towards the end of the season, it became increasingly obvious that he had learned that he wanted to work in an environment where teams and individuals are oriented without reservation towards personal and collective excellence. He began to explain that he now felt more aware of his own special calling, although the precise details of who, when and how were not yet clear. More importantly, he felt both excited and anxious about, 'taking the next step up' to work in a more varied atmosphere of excellence. He described how he had learnt that, the more demanding the challenge, the more important it becomes to strip away all excess baggage and to 'make your life professionally and personally as simple as possible'.

Existential psychology interpretation

The phenomenological framework used to structure the dialogue within this encounter allowed the SP to describe in detail his perceptions and views on how he felt right now. This has been highlighted by Basset-Short and Hammel (1995) as a major strength of the existential approach, in that it encourages a focus on the client's immediate experience. This does not mean that during an existential encounter there is no place to talk about the person's past or indeed their future goals. However, the existential psychologist is asked to maintain a here and now focus and to listen to the client, rather than search for an explanation of the client from their histories or by assessing their aspirations for the future.

It is clear from the case study material considered here, that the SP was wrestling with the key existential issues of meaning. Throughout this phase of the encounter, the dialogue centred on the reflections and experiences of the SP in relation to his understanding of the role expected of him in an elite level professional sport context. This led to a consideration by the SP of what brought him satisfaction and pleasure in his job, and where the dissatisfaction and frustrations were evident. The SP began to dissect his role and clarified that the most important part of this related to his own personal investment in the task. This was contrasted with the more mechanical and functional skills required for success in his role. A recognition and acceptance that the main role for the SP in this environment was that he be 'fully himself' (Kierkegaard, 1844/1944), was truly existential in that it related to the SP's growing awareness that he would have to construct his own meaning of what the role really entailed. Within the encounter, and through working with and alongside the EP, the SP had to confront the normal anxiety which accompanies choice and the act of choosing. The choices of course did not relate to a predetermined list of possibilities. It became clearer to the SP that it was his responsibility to 'take a stand' and that only *he* could do this.

Towards the final part of this phase, the SP provided a rich and detailed account of what he now considered to be the most important meaning of his role. This was articulated by referring to the need to represent a set of values and standards throughout all the demands of his work. The function of the EP, at this stage, was to support the SP in the processes of learning that the search for meaning is a legitimate, vital and essential demand that must not be avoided. It is worth reiterating though that as Spinelli (1996) and Assagioli (1993) have stated, the EP must help their clients to face up to the need to find meaning in their roles and lives as a whole. However, they must not lead or direct the client to what the meaning content should be.

Case study

The SP examined his practices against the specifics of his formal job description. Rather than a detached appraisal, this process led to a focus on effectiveness. This term was being used by the SP to refer to his feelings and thoughts on personal effectiveness rather than an externally focused and quantified interpretation. They discussed that he had struggled to feel effective in enhancing the emotional development of the team. This was explained as being a result of feeling compelled to assist the staff and players to approach their work more strategically, and to attend to detail in planning and preparation.

In addition, the SP described how he had supported and worked closely with the coaching and technical staff. However, in terms of impacting on the players within the team as individuals and collectively, the SP felt that he had maybe been less effective. This comprehensive self-analysis led on to a more detailed consideration of what this meant for the SP and the club. There was clarification that some of this was due to the contextual constraints the SP had to operate within, such as the emotional readiness of players, and the need to address organizational issues around communication and planning. Despite describing some of the players as being content at least to appear somewhat emotionally immature and unprepared to take responsibility at times, the SP felt a powerful sense of regret at having not done enough to meet the deeper needs of those individuals who were more willing to work with him. This progressed to discussion around the need to make the provision of this type of work much more key to his role as a sport psychologist at elite level from now on. At this stage in the SP's own level of professional experience and academic development, he believed that the most important service which could be provided to others in elite level performance environments, would be to operate as a 'sounding board'. This of course is very similar to the idea of clarification which takes place in an existential encounter and depends upon the client.

Finally, the SP talked about the recognition that in his words, 'the higher you go the more simple you need to make your life ... all unnecessary distraction must be cut out!' Further discussion on this revealed that what the SP was describing was the need to protect and 'save yourself', emotionally, physically and mentally. This could only be achieved through self-discipline and by making the logistical and organizational demands of the job as smooth as possible. However, this in turn had provided an opportunity where the SP could find both the time and the emotional energy to throw himself into novel and potentially intimidating experiences where the opportunity to learn was real. The SP clarified that this is what he had encountered over the season during his many visits and meetings with highly successful performers within sport and beyond. This presented itself to the SP as a risk experience, in that there was always some residue of doubt in his mind about the value of these experiences in relation to his role at the club. These were now described on reflection as being of much more importance to the SP in helping him to do his job than almost all other skills and competencies that he already possessed. The SP expressed surprise at this, given that he had never really felt very comfortable to pursue these more difficult (it seemed) to quantify and justify 'study tours'. There had been some anxiety in relation to these experiences because they felt more about the SP's own personal growth and development. Within the encounter with the EP, the SP began to describe how he was now aware that it was through these moments that the SP improved his own self-knowledge. This led to an awareness of how much and what needed to be done at his own club and sports organization to progress towards excellence.

Existential psychology interpretation

It is clear from this account that the SP was clarifying that he was more aware of what Ravizza (2002b) and Moss (1989) have argued in relation to the importance of the person in effecting a change in others. The SP described that despite the tensions and risks inherent in creative activity, it was this dimension rather than a less personal, more controlled and impersonal set of skills, which gave him the deepest sense of confidence and enjoyment in what he was able to bring to the club, individual players and other staff. The feelings of anxiety were associated with the awareness that engaging in creative activities requires the person to fully participate in an act in spite of not knowing if the outcome will be useful or even identifiable! In discussing the importance of creativity, Schneider and May (1995) have argued that from an existential psychology perspective, the creative moment has the power to impact on our deepest core because we can only be creative by 'throwing ourselves unreservedly into the task'. In addition, we are required to stand apart from the task and ourselves and to enter into a process of self-discovery and the discovery of others. When operating creatively, the person is far from being an automaton and yet it does not mean that the focus is self-expression. The SP had taken the decision to expose himself to a range of experiences at other organizations during a demanding time for his own club. He clearly felt guilty about this situation and experienced the normal anxiety that is concomitant with such feelings. The SP described to the EP how he saw himself as caught in a dilemma, where he knew that he needed to gain a broader and more in-depth understanding of himself and his role. This should benefit him as a sport psychologist so that he could assist the club more fully. However, the SP was acutely aware that this action was also aimed at his own self-development and was as much about his growth personally and professionally as it was about improving matters at the club. The SP began to clarify that the failure to confront this tension inherent in the work of a sport psychologist, would lead to an abdication of what they viewed increasingly as their most important role. Put simply and starkly, this could be summed up as a recognition that to be able to help others you must help yourself first! Many of the most important existentially focused therapists such as Von Gebsattel (1954), May (1975) and Frankl (1984) have re-affirmed that the development of personality is the most important task facing the would be therapist or psychologist. What they have in mind is not a set of skills or the accumulation of factual knowledge, important though both of these are, but a level of self-knowledge that can only be won where the whole person engages in something with passion, total commitment, humility and respect. In order to attempt this, the SP described that he had begun to 'prepare the ground' of his own core self by striving to strip away unnecessary baggage and complexity in his professional and personal lives. This relates very closely to the existential ideas of authenticity and presence. Authenticity in our dealings with others is only possible where we have tried to pare the weakness of complexity in our lives so that the strength and depth of simplicity can flourish. This clearing away process is paradoxically often best achieved through placing ourselves in situations where the gap between where we are and what we do is clearly visible in comparison to what we can pursue, and must do to grow and develop. The SP's brief but intense immersions in the lives and work of others operating at the very highest levels of professional sport, brought the uncomfortable experience of angst or normal anxiety. However, alongside this there was an increasing awareness that these experiences were capable of helping the SP to confront thoughts about how effective he was currently, and what he needed to do to work in more advanced and demanding environments in the future. From an existential psychology approach, the normal anxiety experienced by the SP can be viewed as beneficial where the person is prepared to move forward in their development rather than shrinking from the challenge.

7   Ethical issues in existential practice
Authentic values and personal responsibility

Introduction

Any mention of values may seem incompatible with the idea of psychology as a science. Advocates of a reductionist and positivistic psychology, founded on the tenets of natural science, reject outright the possibility that psychology can legitimately offer us anything about values. Giorgi (1985) has challenged the validity of this stance and has pointed out that this represents a value position in itself.

Existential psychologists like Schneider and May (1995) and those arguing for a human science approach to the discipline (Giorgi, 1970), have posited that anxiety is only possible because the human is a valuing being. They contend that anxiety is experienced when something that is important and valued by us is threatened. According to this view, values are always under constant threat and gain in depth and maturity as we confront the choices and make decisions in our lives. Existential psychology following Kierkegaard and others has claimed that anxiety is the emotion associated with a threat to those values which one holds dear. Such deeply held values are said to form the centre of a person, or their core self. A striking example of the importance of values can be seen where a person or group may be more prepared to face annihilation rather than relinquish their beliefs and deeply held values. On this point, existential psychology has been highly critical of contemporary society at least in the West. They have suggested that very few people seem prepared to face anxiety and remain true to their values. This situation, it is proposed, is due to the self-alienation and large scale personal disintegration and individual neurosis which has been a feature of modern life. Finally on this point, May (1967) has stated that an individual's capacity to meet anxiety positively is directly related to the adequacy of their value system. The individual without healthy and strong values will attempt to avoid anxiety by either falling into line with the views of others, trying to ignore their claims by engaging in constant activity, or by crystallizing their values into rigid dogma. All of these strategies can lead to a weakening of the core self and stagnation in terms of personal growth. Where this cycle repeats itself frequently, there is the danger of neurotic anxiety, which May (1967: 80) described as something that, 'develops when a person has been unable to meet normal anxiety at the time of the actual crisis in his growth and the threat to his [*values*]'.

Given this emphasis on the importance of values, it seems likely that an existential view might stress that developing mature and sound values would assist a sports performer to deal with the normal anxiety encountered in sport. This can be better understood if it is remembered that the concern is not only with performance or competitive anxiety, but also with the experience of this emotion throughout all aspects of our lives. However, for the sport psychologist the question of values and ethical behaviour is arguably of even greater importance. This applies to all psychologists and therapists, but even more so to existential practitioners because of their claim that who you are is more important than what you use when working in applied settings.

Finally, it is important to identify what type of values the existential psychologists are referring to. According to May (1977), values are formed and developed as the individual grows and matures. The first values that the child acquires relate to our lower needs such as care, food and security. Later on, values are based on the need for peer approval and achievement. These categories of value are very similar to the lower order needs identified by humanistic psychologists such as Maslow (1954). The existential notion of mature values differs quite significantly from Maslow's concept of self-actualization, which they have tended to criticize as being excessively self and not other focused. May (1967: 82) describes mature values as those that:

> transcend also the immediate in-group, and extend outward toward the good of the community, ideally and ultimately embracing humanity as a whole ... The more mature a man's values are, the less it matters to him whether his values are literally satisfied or not. The satisfaction and security lie in the holding of values.
>
> May (1967: 82)

As the healthy person develops and matures, their values are transformed and begin to take on a largely symbolic character. Such values may be represented by a belief in the essential goodness of humanity, a belief in freedom or a commitment to God. In each case, the value must be personally grasped by the individual and made their own through their total engagement in the situation. An adequate system of values will allow the individual to be inner directed and future oriented. The existential view argues that it is through the accumulation of these types of values that a person is able to experience hope and to commit to some future course of action. Finally, they contend that as healthy and mature values are freely chosen, they bring responsibility. This results in the need to accept that it is in holding on to these hard won values that we can develop a deep sense of self; one which is little affected by the views our peers and others have of us.

The following case study highlights how a sport psychologist (SP), operating in an elite level team setting, attempts to deliver a service in a number of ethically difficult situations. These present the SP with an opportunity to make particular choices and take decisions that he is willing to defend. According to existential psychotherapists such as Frankl (1984), the task facing the individual is to simultaneously maintain openness to others without abandoning or diluting their most personal and deeply held values. This makes considerable demands upon the psychologist working in an environment where the dominant values are those centred on self-preservation and material gain.

Case study

The SP had been contracted for a season to deliver a dedicated sport psychology service to the first team of a professional football club. The sports organization was a very high profile, wealthy and media friendly club. The top players were highly paid internationals and many of the younger less experienced team members were high profile individuals.

The SP described how he had wrestled with the different standards and expectations that others held about providing a high quality service. He explained how the dominant culture at the football club was one of detached and cynical pragmatism. This seemed to have a direct impact on the playing, coaching and other support staff; a mood of self-interest and passive conformity was clearly evident. Within this context, the SP attempted to improve internal communication, develop team dynamics and counsel individual first team players. This final task involved delivery of some MST. The greater part of his role though related to providing counselling for individual players in formal and informal settings. These sessions and encounters were concerned with helping players to improve their sports performances, however, the issues discussed ranged from more narrowly focused match day and training matters to broader life concerns. The approach adopted by the SP was largely informed by existential psychology. Attention was directed at the key existential themes and the work was conceived holistically. The SP encountered considerable resistance from many players and some senior staff at times, in terms of what he was trying to do. He was subject to abrasive and immature behaviour, and a constant undercurrent of negativity and criticism as he attempted to offer a sport psychology service. There was a significant feeling of resentment expressed by a small but influential cadre of staff and players towards the SP personally. This was largely due to the contrast between his motivation and enthusiasm to work hard in his role, and the apathetic and complacent behaviour demonstrated by some colleagues. The club and sports organization itself was shrouded in a mood of despair and despondency as a result of financial problems and a lack of success on the field.

It became apparent that the culture of the club supported mediocrity. Those players and staff who showed a tendency to strive to improve, and better themselves were shunned and ridiculed in a 'footballing' culture, where an attempt to improve was seen as almost mutinous because it threatened the comfort zone of the group.

Ethical decisions and discerning values

One of the ethical problems presented in the scenario just outlined is how a sport psychologist can remain true to values such as integrity and honesty, where the cultural norm is largely one of dishonesty and selfishness. At a more prosaic level, the issue facing the SP relates to how much and what they are prepared to compromise or abandon in order to work with people that have a very different set of values. The SP was confronted by this ethical dilemma in his dealings with both the players and his non-playing colleagues. From a practical perspective, this issue was addressed by eventually making a choice to only work with those who were willing to support the approach. This decision was taken when the SP had reviewed his own practices, and after a period of intense reflection on his work and his own values and standards. This self-reflection was assisted through contact with a small number of experienced and trusted advisors and friends, and by engaging in several conversations and encounters with an existential psychologist (EP). This was considered an important part of the process which he engaged in throughout his period at the club. The encounters with the EP provided an opportunity to re-examine the situation that the SP was operating within and to face up to the anxiety associated with delivering a service in an ethical way, within a distinctly unethical environment. The EP provided written accounts of each meeting for the SP to assist a deeper level of reflection, and to enable the dialogue between each person to become ever more authentic and real. Indeed, on this last point, the SP was able to articulate that the main benefit of encounters with the EP and the discussions with close friends was to help him to return to a consideration of 'reality'. This term relates to the existential idea of the *Lebenswelt*, or the world-as-lived. This describes that in order to cut through and past the inauthentic nature of much of what passes for communication between people, it is necessary to go direct to the language of pre-reflection. That is, reality can be accessed, however, it is rarely revealed in the words of people and organizations except when they express themselves unguardedly, and without reservation. This involved a careful explanation of what was said at the club and during the SP's dealings with others. This revealed that the reality for players and some staff was that the repeated failure to confront the anxiety associated with accepting some responsibility for the currently perilous position of the club, had now given way to something more in common with neurotic anxiety. Players chose to deny their responsibility for their performance on the field, preferring to blame the situation, circumstances and other people. In other words, there were many in the team who had sought refuge from the discomfort of anxiety. They achieved this through disengaging from their role as professional athletes and in seeking to escape by merging into the rest of the team. This of course is the most effective way to remain in a particular role but as Kierkegaard (1844/1944) has pointed out, it is acquired at the great cost of a diminishing self. In this way, the SP was able to recognize that the team contained for the most part, players with 'stunted personal centres' (Buber, 1970: 178–179); when what was needed were strong personalities prepared to courageously accept their part, and to throw themselves into the task both as individuals and collectively.

The SP made a choice to continue to work with everyone, and to offer a service aimed at encouraging authenticity, personal growth and existential courage. However, increasingly the SP found himself becoming more isolated, and unable to work with players and key staff due to their refusal to become involved in the process. The SP decided that it was ethically correct to continue to work with those members of staff and players that remained open to his approach. This is consistent with one of the most important values of the existential psychology approach. According to Marcel, this requires the therapist to maintain a 'state of availability or receptiveness (Disponibilité) ... Which is creative in its fidelity to what life presents' (Moss, 1989: 200). One of the most important values in the existentialism of Kierkegaard and Marcel is that persons should be viewed and treated as ends. Or put another way, values should not be based on either an abstract notion of what constitutes a human being, or on a materialist conception, that considers us in terms of efficiency. Instead, as Marcel has affirmed, the values to be recognized are freedom, faith, love, humility, courage and justice. However, these should not be conceived in conceptual terms first (as Sartre would argue) but gain real meaning only as they are lived out in our daily lives. This approach represents a complete rejection of any attempt to scientifically determine a system of values. The existential psychologist following the formulations of its modern founder, Kierkegaard, is warned against the pride of creating values and instead is told to use creativity to help them to grasp the universal values of life. These of course may present themselves to us in a range of styles but their substance remains immutable and eternally valid.

Case study

The SP described how he had set aside an increasingly significant period of time to reflect upon his philosophy of practice and values. These were summed up as being about integrity, pride, responsibility, honesty, compassion and passion. The SP revisited academic literature in psychology, sport and philosophy to anchor these values more firmly and deeply into his consciousness. There was also a concerted effort from the SP to resist what he referred to as the slow, steady yet subtle drift towards the brittle inauthentic values, and unethical attitudes and behaviours prevailing in the club. He described this to the EP in terms of 'rowing against a powerful, slow moving river'. In order to keep rowing up stream he had to accept that he would have to do this largely on his own. As the season progressed the mood in the team and situation with the club deteriorated further. The SP felt a strong pull to accept that nothing could be done to positively change matters. Those around him had for the most part given up trying to perform their jobs and roles fully, and advised the SP to do the bare minimum and to look after himself first! This led the SP to a phase of in-depth personal evaluation, which resulted in even greater commitment to delivering his service in an uncompromising and clear manner. This action brought a considerable range of negative reactions from several key staff and players at the club. The SP outlined to the EP that although these objections to his work emerged in different ways, his response to them as a whole was consistent and uniform. However, there were notable successes with those players who remained open and receptive to the SP's approach. He described that he had been able to withstand this uncomfortable period by developing a deeper awareness of his own practice of sport psychology. This had also resulted in a period of sustained scrutiny of the ethical maxims and values that underpinned his work. The end product of this was that it enhanced his commitment to operating in a particular way despite the very many obstacles and difficulties he encountered because of this.

Existential ethics

An existential psychology account of the experience of the SP during this period would emphasize the importance of what Bassett-Short and Hammel (1995: 128) have called, 'an acknowledgement of the limits of action'. This is relevant to both clients and psychologists, and stresses that the capacity for choice is always constrained by the contextual settings. It is quite evident that the SP increasingly came to recognize that much of what he wanted to do could not be delivered in this environment. A value based ethical decision had to be made to choose a particular course of action. The SP began to reflect on his professional practice, and to reaffirm the values and personal philosophy to which he was committed. Despite the accompanying anxiety, he chose to continue to offer a service to players and staff albeit unwelcome for the most part. According to the existential psychology view, making choices like these in the face of considerable difficulty and opposition can serve to enhance the deepest human qualities of the person. This echoes the claims of those in sport psychology (Corlett, 1996; Salter, 1997; Nesti, 2002) who have argued that the development of self-knowledge is the most important task facing the client-athlete and the psychologist. This ethical decision has been captured in a most profound and powerful way by Frankl, when writing about his experiences in a concentration camp during World War II. Frankl has claimed that even in the most destructive and powerless environments one thing remains, 'the last of the human freedoms – to choose one's attitude in any given set of circumstances, to choose one's own way . . . in this case, to avoid being moulded into the form of the typical inmate' (Frankl, 1984: 75).

The SP's choice did not come at this type of cost, but it did require him to adopt a stance (i.e. make an ethical decision and act upon it) based on key existential values. In its wake, this choice brought the SP into direct conflict with the values of his employer and led to a painful experience of isolation and a sense of alienation. However, by his refusal to conform to the opinions of the group, the SP maintained and strengthened his authenticity. Armed with this, he returned renewed and re-invigorated in his deepest core self and was able to continue to offer his service to those prepared to engage. In terms of the players, this meant that his work was now restricted to only those few individuals who were prepared to accept reality, and begin to acknowledge that they were partly responsible for the plight of the team and the club as a whole.

Case study

Towards the end of the encounter with the EP, the SP began to describe how he viewed his own situation, the end of a very unsuccessful season for the team and the club as a whole. The SP stated that all of his thoughts were future orientated and that increasingly he was spending time reflecting on a new start outside of elite professional football. He had spent a year during which he had experienced, directly and indirectly, feelings of resentment from some colleagues and players in relation to his efforts to improve the team and support individuals within the club. This led to a very detailed account of how he found himself being prepared to make the most of this unappealing and frustrating aspect of his role. The SP articulated how he spontaneously adapted his demeanour at the club to allow him to behave in a way which was congruent with the perception that (some) others held of him. Nevertheless, he talked about being very aware during this period that he did not want to work in this type of environment long term. This reflection had to be masked during most of his dealings with players and other staff, however, he now felt angry that the team had been relegated from the league and that few had seemed truly upset by the likelihood of this along the way. This led to a description of how he had gone through a range of emotions throughout the season, and that he had learned to deal with these after spending a great deal of energy on trying to devise ways to improve matters at the club and the performance of the team. The SP explained that after trying to work against a culture of complacency, the pain of failure and defeat became numb. This was contrasted with how he felt about the reserve team at the club. This collection of individuals cared deeply and the SP developed a strong relationship with them. He felt that he was able to achieve much with this group both in physical and psychological terms, and that he contributed towards their Premier Division Championship victory. This led to a discussion around the differences between investing his self fully and authentically in the work with one set of players, and eventually merely fulfilling his professional responsibilities with the first team. Throughout the year, the SP had decided to keep a detailed diary containing his reflections on his feelings and accounts of the different vignettes he experienced daily. He discussed that the meetings, which he had with his training supervisor, were most beneficial in terms of providing the opportunity to clarify the experiences that he was having at the club. In particular, the SP emphasized that it was important to have these encounters, and to have frequent dialogue with two very experienced and trusted mentors who were working at other clubs in professional football. These three people helped the SP to gain support for what he was attempting to achieve at the club, and to develop a deeper and more committed understanding of what he viewed as his role. The SP stressed that these discussions did not focus on specific tasks or involve a systematic analysis of the service he was supposed to offer based on his job description. The SP explained to the EP that the encounters with his supervisor and communication with mentors really only addressed two important themes. The SP described that the completion of a diary was an attempt to help him to remain focused on reality. This was articulated as 'the truth behind the façade and games of deception' that the SP encountered in many of his dealings on a daily basis. The other major theme was that he began to clarify what he needed to do to allow him to offer a sport psychology service in such a difficult environment. He described that he spent a considerable period of time reflecting on who he was, rather than what he needed to do or on how this should be done. This was a major surprise to him because he had anticipated that with his lack of experience in the milieu of elite level professional football, his biggest challenge would relate to the skills and strategies which he needed to acquire to do his job effectively. It became ever clearer to him as the season progressed that to 'survive and come out of the other end' he needed to know who he was and what he stood for. This was very unexpected according to the SP. He had expected that he would have little need and even less time to devote to a serious consideration of this, and that this demand for self-knowledge would only reveal itself, if at all, when his active role was over (i.e. at the season's end). The SP stated that the major focus in this regard was to consider what he felt were his core values, and to bring these much more clearly to bear on his work. This was described as a difficult, exciting and yet painful experience. The SP explained to the EP that he had reacted to the largely negative environment at the club by clearly revealing his views and opinions on a range of matters. He reflected that this made him feel a little uneasy at times and that he felt compelled to act this way, even though he would have preferred to adopt a more subtle and withdrawn approach in this respect. He explained that this was because he felt divided in terms of wanting to present a set of values through his own behaviour, whilst not being very sure about what these values were in the first place. In addition, the SP felt uncomfortable in having to confront people in such a direct way with what he expected, and the values and ethics underpinning his actions. He described that he was constantly aware that this way of working made it easier for others to reject his support service and to further undermine his role at the club. The SP claimed that he spent a much greater time than he had anticipated before his appointment reflecting on his values and beliefs, and on what he called the need to, 'remain true to your most deeply held values and views on ethical behaviour without selling out!' This led to an awareness that it was important in the environment of elite professional football to hold fast to your own values. Alongside of this, the SP needed to be capable of presenting these values in a diluted form to those that seemed so threatened and anxious by them as they were encountered in their daily activities.

Existential interpretation: authenticity, values and ethical action

According to Cohn (1997: 122), 'the aim of existential psychotherapy is often described as the emergence of a more authentic way of living'. The term *authenticity* implies that something or someone is capable of being real. Another way of expressing this is that we are divided into a 'false self' and a 'true self'. However, from an existential psychology view, this division must be understood as fluid. From a phenomenological perspective it is also inappropriate to accept such a strict dualistic conception. Nevertheless, the existential approach highlights that our task remains one of becoming more authentic. This is easier to understand in terms of the need to be true to yourself rather than allowing your values, views and behaviour to be based on what others say. This of course does not mean that authentic behaviour and values must be singular and not informed by the world beyond the individual. However, the test of authenticity is that they must, amongst these other things, have been grasped personally by an individual and fought for, rather than being dispassionately assimilated.

It is clear from the case study that the SP was striving to meet the challenges associated with authenticity. The discussions with other mentors and the EP were concerned with clarification of the appropriateness of this action, and crucially provided an opportunity to examine the values guiding his work as an applied sport psychologist. It became increasingly clear to him that although he had not anticipated this at the start of his job, the need to review and commit personally to a set of values became a major task facing the SP.

All of this relates to the difficult to grasp existential idea of *Dasein*, or Being-in-the-world. Following Heidegger, the existentialist approach emphasizes that we are constantly engaged in a project in our lives where, we can only really know ourselves in relation to those things and other persons we are involved with. This involvement, which is better described as concern or care, is something that influences our level of openness to the world and our response to it. Therefore to be authentic, really requires a person to deal with reality as such and to ignore the at times, powerful and almost totalitarian call emanating from our idealized 'inner' selves. Through our Being-in-the-world, we are inevitably faced with the need to accept that we are required to choose our own ways of responding to the givens of existence. These 'givens' refer to the existential facts confronting us as human beings, such as the inevitability of death, our relations with others and our embodiment. It is, 'between the "givens" of existence and our response to them' (Cohn, 1997: 125) that we have the potential for growth and action, or despair and impassivity. Where this is not faced by the individual person, there is the possibility that psychological disturbance and genuinely clinical factors will emerge. However, the SP in this situation wrestled with this dynamic continuously from the earliest phases of his work at the club. He strived to grow in authenticity through facing up to the need to clarify his own values more fully and to remain true to these despite the anxiety experienced as a result of this. In doing this, he avoided the fate of so many individuals who in abdicating their obligation to choose and by ignoring the call to participate in the recognition of mature values, experience what Sartre referred to as *bad faith*. This has been explained precisely by Cannon (1991: 46), as taking one or both of the two dishonest positions about reality: 'If I pretend either to be free in a world without facts or to be a fact in a world without freedom.' If we replace the term facts for values, or indeed any other foundational element governing our behaviour, it becomes clear that mature values would be those which are based on truth, and yet would only be real where we were active in grafting these into our own unique situations. The SP was prepared to face up to this existential demand and decided to accept the anxiety associated with following his values in an environment with a very different set of values. Failure to do this can lead to existential guilt (May, 1977) and if pursued continuously, can result in clinical problems for an individual. It is striking that the SP tried to accept that he was operating in a significantly unethical setting where the dominant values were based on egocentric needs and material gain. He attempted to accept that he needed to find and allow his values to impact on all of his activities at the club. In doing this he has had to stay on what Buber (1970) has called the 'narrow ridge' that exists between idealization and wishful thinking on one side, and despair and a feeling of paralysis on the other. The quest towards authenticity requires considerable courage. The SP had to closely examine his values and decide to act in accordance with them knowing that his life and role would be more difficult as a result. This creative process can only be undertaken where a person accepts with courage that they must 'become' their values as it were. The person must not shrink from this task despite the knowledge that they will be unable to achieve this perfect synthesis between their actions and values. This point also connects to the issue of normative behaviour. According to existential psychologists, the process towards authenticity and authentic values is always an incomplete project. Further to this, there is no measure of how much authenticity a person needs to achieve because the focus should be on the never-ending pursuit of this, against the weight of the world that tries to keep the individual in the chains of inauthenticity.

8 To be or not to be . . .

. . . an existential sport psychologist?

Introduction

There are many reasons why a sport psychologist will elect to carry out their research or applied work from a particular psychological approach. Some of the most important relate to education and training, whether the focus is on research or practical work, and the level and performance demands of the athlete the sport psychologist is working with. These factors and other more individually significant explanations will be considered in this final chapter. This will be attempted through a critical self-analysis of how the author developed an interest in existential psychology approaches during fifteen years as a British Association of Sport and Exercise Sciences (BASES) accredited sport and exercise psychologist.

It could be argued that sport psychology is now a well-established and recognized academic discipline. There has been a rapid and sizeable increase in research in the area and an expansion of sport and exercise psychology courses within university and further education sectors. During this time, the opportunities to work in applied settings in sport have also increased. This has taken place due to several developments, however, there are three of these which could be viewed as most important. First, there has been much greater publicity given to the centrality of the mind in sports performance. Media reports, coaching publications and personal testimonies from coaches, managers and athletes at the highest levels of sport frequently emphasize that motivation, focus and other psychological elements are crucial to success. It has become much less likely that sport psychology will be viewed negatively by coaches in particular. Most accept that sport psychologists can provide a complimentary role and offer additional expertise in a specific and key area. This has been helped because of the decision of many governing bodies of sports and national coaching organizations (e.g. UK Sports Coach) to include sport psychology within their coaching awards. These developments during the past decade have finally removed the misunderstanding that many held previously, that sport psychology was only for those suffering from clinical problems (Andersen, 2000).

Second, as far back as 1987, Martens noted that sport psychology had built up an extensive and impressive corpus of scientific work. Although he warned that there remained a greater need to engage in more ecologically valid research in the field (Martens, 1979), and to consider other approaches beyond the positivistic paradigm, Martens acknowledged just how far the discipline had come in such a short time. Of course, there are still critical voices (Salter, 1997; Nesti, 2002) who argue that Martens' earlier call has gone largely unheeded. Nevertheless, within academia and at the higher levels of coaching, there has been a recognition that a vast scientific body of academic work and studies in sport psychology has been established. This has undoubtedly led to more awareness of the study of sport psychology by mainstream applied and research psychologists. In some institutions this has also given rise to a cross fertilization of ideas between sport psychology and psychology, and has resulted in several notable examples of collaboration. For example, in the UK Cockerill's (2002) applied text on sport psychology features contributions in equal measure from sport psychologists and mainstream psychologists interested in sport. At a professional and organizational level, the British Psychological Society (BPS) has a sport and exercise section and there exists a strong level of mutual support and co-operation between this and the more numerous grouping within BASES.

Finally, it has been noted that we are living in an age where there is a huge interest in all things psychological. There are a range of plausible explanations for this, each reflecting whether it is viewed as a welcome development or a negative phenomenon. Arguably, one of the most compelling explanations has been offered by Pieper (1989). He suggests that during an historical period when the traditional structures of community have largely disintegrated or been abandoned, it is understandable that individuals turn to anything that can promise to help them negotiate a successful way through their lives. The outcome of this as far as sport psychology is concerned, is that there is a more positive climate towards psychology and a greater acceptance that people can improve their effectiveness through their own efforts. Against this backdrop, it is easier to understand how MST and the use of psychological techniques in sport are much more readily accepted by performers and coaches at all levels.

These broad contextual factors have had a major impact on the generally positive view held by many individuals and organizations on the importance of the mental side in competitive sport in particular. However, on the down side, this enthusiasm for sport psychology has not always resulted in satisfied athletes and positive changes in performance behaviour. There are numerous possible explanations for this situation. Some of the most clearly documented relate to issues around adherence to MST (Bull and Shambrook, 1998), weaknesses in evaluation of programmes (Anderson *et al.*, 2002), failure to individualize interventions (Jones and Hardy, 1990) and ignoring broader life concerns facing athletes (Nesti and Sewell, 1997). Beyond the findings of traditional sport psychology research, there have been suggestions that the discipline is often unable to assist sports performers because it is failing to address the most important psychological issues. Corlett (1996) has cogently argued that the key task facing the sport psychologist is to assist the development of self-knowledge in the sports performer. He has suggested that it is by this process, an athlete will be able to improve their competitive sports performance, and learn skills and acquire knowledge that will be vital to their lives outside sport.

This chapter considers some of the possible implications for sport psychology and sport psychologists arising from the views of Corlett (1996) and Salter (1997) in relation to the different views of the majority, who despite claims to the contrary, remain convinced that sport psychology is primarily about mental skills and teaching psychological techniques. In order to enter into the centre of this debate, it may be helpful to examine how these issues were experienced and encountered by the author during his work in sport psychology.

Meeting with reality

The requirement to focus on reality is something which separates existential psychology from other approaches within the discipline. In very simple terms, 'reality' refers to what we might call our true lives; something we experience without the need to reflect upon, theorize about, or view as a project apart from ourselves. This difficult, obscure and important existential idea, can easily be ignored or forgotten when we decide to look at the life or situation of someone else. When in this position, it is hard not to approach the other person as if they were in fact a task facing us, just as we might do when confronted with a material object. During this frame of mind it is possible to adopt the natural attitude (see Chapter 2), and begin to lose oneself and the other individual in an analysis of their attitudes, motivations, emotions and plans. Where we do this we are no longer attending to 'reality' the real lived life of the person before us, but instead have abandoned reality to enter the domain of specu-lation, hypothesis testing and theorizing. According to existential psychology, we must attempt to remain in the world of reality for as long as possible when we approach another person in research or applied settings. Theorizing and the rest of it are legitimate activities for us but only after our encounter with a person. Although most existential psychologists are uncomfortable with the idea of research models and theory, this probably reflects their desire to ensure that direct, spontaneous and authentic dialogue can take place between persons.

Personal reflections

As a sport psychologist working with a disparate group of athletes, I would often attempt to get performers to describe how they became involved in their sport and to detail their achievements. This approach was used as an 'ice breaker' and to gather background information on the client. The idea was to help the session to remain focused on the most important and personally significant aspects of the athlete's sporting life. Over the years I recognized that whilst clients seemed to enjoy talking about themselves in this way, they sometimes appeared to be waiting for me to interject at various points to offer a solution, or to re-phrase their thoughts using psychological terms and technical language.

Particularly with more reticent and less verbally fluent clients and with younger performers, I found that I struggled to avoid the temptation to theorize and offer possible strategies. After these encounters, my written notes would often reveal that the dialogue had remained focused on the 'real' at the beginning and during the last few minutes of sessions. However, during some of the 30–40 minutes in between times, I had taken control of the session and provided theoretical and technical accounts of what I thought was happening and what I felt they needed to do next.

Existential psychology approaches may not be easy to use with young, inexperienced athletes or those with weak communication skills. This point is rarely addressed in most texts on existential psychology. Some existential-phenomenologists have stated that this method requires that research participants have good interpersonal skills and are self-aware. Taken to the extreme, this could mean that only a small group of sports performers would be able to benefit from the existential approach. This would ignore two very important facts of existential psychology: the use of silence and the power of presence. For example, within an encounter with a young athlete or with someone who is reluctant to talk about themselves, their feelings or an event, the presence of the sport psychologist can facilitate a participation in the session which goes beyond the verbal and non-verbal forms of communication. This capacity to remain with the reality of a client's life, no matter how poorly this is described verbally, depends on the sport psychologist seeing the athlete as a person and not an individual. Buber (1958) has explained that this is only possible where the sport psychologist or counsellor strives continually to approach the other as a *Thou* rather that an *it*. The I-Thou mode involves a deeply personal level of communication where there is an unguarded self-giving of one person to another. The capacity to achieve this depends upon the personality of the counsellor and in particular on their ability to remain present to the other person in what Marcel (1948) called an attitude of 'disponibilité' or spiritual availability.

In terms of the use of silence, Spinelli (1996) has suggested that the psychologist within an existential encounter must allow these often uncomfortable and anxiety producing moments to run their course. He warns that by 'jumping in' too early during these moments, the sport psychologist may inadvertently prevent deeper reflection in the client and stifle the beginnings of some acceptance of their own freedom to act.

This can be better understood where we keep in mind that the existential psychology based sport psychology session is not about making the client feel comfortable, but with helping them to face up to the anxiety associated with thinking for themselves and making choices. During my initial years as a sport psychologist, I often anaesthetized the feeling of anxiety that accompanied silent moments in an encounter. This was mainly due to my failure to face the interpersonal discomfort associated with these periods and because of a desire to provide an 'expert's' solution to the issues discussed. The result of course, was that frequently very little was achieved because I had allowed the session to stray from a consideration of reality, towards the more banal and impersonal world of abstract speculation and quick fix technical pseudo-solutions!

However, it should be noted that there is the possibility that this approach will fail to use a specific mental skill technique, such as goal setting or visualization, where this could assist the athlete, at least in the short term. During some of my earliest work with young performers and those who struggled to verbalize what they were experiencing, I would teach psychological skills within individual sessions primarily to build a relationship and develop trust. Adherence to MST within this context became much less of a focus. Although the lack of adherence could lead to frustration at times for both the sport psychologist and the performer, I began to understand more fully that I needed to be continually vigilant about the use of psychological techniques within my work. Existential psychology accepts that techniques can be utilized especially within time-limited therapy (Cooper, 2003). However, it warns that these can only be used as a small part of the process of working with someone and in one sense, should be a matter of last resort. This is because techniques can deflect the athlete and the sport psychologist from keeping a focus on the reality of what a person is experiencing, and could result in attention being diverted towards dealing with symptoms.

I found that the challenge to remain with the reality of the athlete's lived world was not related to my lack of understanding about the importance of this. Instead, I was able to reflect that the more important issue for me was that I found it very hard to completely withdraw from the natural science attitude, which had been the main approach I had been exposed to throughout my education and training in sport psychology. Fortunately, a grounding in existential psychology and an awareness of other person centred approaches, acquired during postgraduate mainstream psychology courses and research, provided me with something very different to the dominant cognitive–behavioural approach in traditional sport psychology. In addition, as my work progressed I began to observe through analysis of my case notes, client reports and face-to-face communication with the sports performers themselves, that my most effective work occurred where I had been able to stay with the *person*, rather than trying to help them psychologically. This genuine learning (Collaizzi, 1978) emerged slowly and painfully after periods of self-doubt about how active and directive I should be in encounters with individual sports performers. As I started to reduce the use of MST within my work, two very important factors became much clearer to me. Firstly, I recognized that the continued incorporation of psychological techniques in my applied work interfered with the often painful (because personal) consideration of the real lived world of the performer. Secondly, it helped me to see that I had often employed some MST within my work because it allowed me to adopt a more directive and targeted approach with the client. This helped me to review the literature (e.g. Maslow, 1968; Spinelli, 1989; Cooper, 2003) that delineated the key differences between humanistic and other person centred approaches to counselling and existential psychology.

Through this process, I was able to rediscover that my approach had more in common with the existential psychology espoused by May (1977), Frankl (1984) and Yalom (1999), and the historical and philosophical existentialism within Kierkegaard, Marcel and Aquinas. This placed my existential sport psychology practice at odds with the person centred humanistic psychologists and the nihilistic existentialism of Sartre and those following more post-modernist approaches such as Cooper (2003). This truly existential self-encounter has been an ongoing process. It is no more than what I have been asking my clients to do, which is to constantly engage in self-reflection and critical analysis, and to take a stand, time and again, in relation to the existential need to discover meaning in their daily lives.

I began to grasp an important issue after discussing with a colleague about my own particular way of operating existentially. I clarified that MST in particular, had represented a fairly important part of my earlier work with athletes because through it, I was able to assume a more authoritative and directive style. I began to greatly diminish my use of MST in encounters with sports performers only after I rediscovered that more confrontational and directive modes of practice were viewed positively within the work of a disparate group of existential psychologists (e.g. Frankl, 1984; Van Deurzen-Smith, 2002). I became much more comfortable with the need to adopt a more provocative, challenging and confrontational style with my clients in relation to what Yalom (1980) identified as the major existential concerns of death, meaninglessness, freedom and isolation. This development and the changes with my practice was informed by the material provided by clients and from intense reflections upon my own view of reality. Although this view contains much that is shared by others, it is also unique and individual at the same time because it is personal and has been appropriated by me through my own existential journey in life. These views have become sharper during more recent years working with sports performers. This has led to a closer synergy between what existentialism and the ideas of existential psychology mean in the reality of my professional and personal life, and the lived world of my clients.

The careful use of a more direct and confrontational approach alongside genuine empathy and striving to stay present to the other person in an encounter, has proved to be a valuable addition to my work with athletes. This has been especially so when facing the normal anxiety experienced as a by-product of individual growth and facing the challenges of everyday life. This led to renewed study of the earlier existential ideas of Kierkegaard and I attempted to more closely integrate his perspective into my own work in sport. As a result, my approach has evolved into something with a sharp edge – a person centred approach with attitude! Given that the reality of many sports performers' lives is about learning new skills and performing under pressure, a more Kierkegaardian approach to sport psychology counselling appealed to many at all levels of performance (as long as they were serious about their sport and it had an important place in their lives). Such a shift towards a more blunt and hard hitting style, alongside a genuine attempt to meet the other as a person and not an individual, was consistent with much of what Kierkegaard (1844/1944) had offered on this subject over 150 years before. His argument was:

> that the growth of a person or, as he terms it, a self, occurs by *facing up to* and moving through normal anxiety. In this way the person is better pre-pared to face the experience of anxiety again, and as this process is repeated through life, individuals teach themselves faith and courage, and will be able to face their freedom and life, rather than devoting energies to evading anxiety experiences. This is particularly important because as Kierkegaard has argued, making choices, taking decisions and at a deeper level, being creative always involves the experience of anxiety.
>
> (Nesti, 2001: 207)

Engaging in sport psychology work with athletes during the past 15 years has helped me to reformulate my understanding of existential psychology and to reconfigure my approach to applied practice. The existential search for the ultimate approach is a never-ending one. For many psychologists and sport psychologists, such a view would be unacceptable on several grounds, not the least of which is that it is an admission that the approach you choose should always be a 'work in progress!'

However, at a different level, this resonates with the claims of Cooper who suggests that:

> Just as there is no one way of being an existential thinker, so there is no one way of being an existential therapist, and it is this very diversity and difference that is the life-blood of the existential therapeutic field.
>
> Cooper (2003: 151)

Is it all talk?

Most existential psychology approaches are reluctant to rely on psychological techniques in their work. This applies equally within an encounter itself and to any work beyond this. However, a closer examination of the work of Frankl (1984) and psychoanalytically oriented therapists such as Schneider (1995) shows that techniques can be quite an important tool for some existentially inclined psychologists which the therapist can use within their sessions.

The general tendency to diminish the role of psychological techniques within any type of existential encounter between two persons is very different to the situation in sport psychology. Despite several and repeated calls to con-sider the importance of more than MST in our applied work, little seems to have happened. This can easily be seen from the continued interest in MST related research at sport psychology conferences, in peer-reviewed journals and in most undergraduate texts in the field. A survey of these developments would suggest that despite the calls of Corlett (1996) and Salter (1997), applied sport psychology remains largely synonymous with MST. In recent years there have been attempts to broaden the area to consider the use of Reversal theory (Kerr, 2001), Performance profiling (Butler, 1997) and humanistic approaches (Hill, 2001) to counselling athletes. However, the dominant approach within the training and education of sport psychology students remains that of MST, which is for the most part based on a cognitive–behavioural model. There has been some recognition that much of the reality of providing one-to-one support with sports performers is that MST often represents an insignificant element. The work of Anderson (2000) and Petipas *et al.* (1996), considers the contribution that counselling theory can make in applied work with sports performers. This has helped to close the gap between traditional academic sport psychology and applied practice. Unfortunately, much of the literature is still lacking in terms of providing a strong theoretical underpinning to what is being discussed. Readers are often left with the impression that counselling, life development and life skills approaches are primarily concerned with communication and using counselling skills. Such a view is unhelpful and inaccurate because counselling psychology, which according to Woolfe (1996) is based mostly on a humanistic psychology person centred paradigm, has an extensive and impressive theoretical and academic base. Given the failure to acknowledge this, it becomes more easy to understand that for many sport psychologists the choice is between MST or just talking! Indeed there are applied sport psychologists who are apparently completely unaware that there are many established and competing views on how to talk to someone in a counselling, therapeutic or clinical setting. It is slowly being addressed through recent publications on counselling in sport settings (Lavallee and Cockerill, 2002) and through graduate sport psychology training programmes. One excellent example of this is the sport psychology counselling course at JFK University in the USA where postgraduate students cover areas such as models of counselling and their application to sport and exercise psychology. However, this remains very much the exception and the common view continues to be that what sport psychologists do beyond MST in their sessions is engage in building trust, enhancing communication and developing a relationship with the client by 'just talking'. There is little doubt that some sport psychologists can do very effective work this way, and possess outstanding abilities as communicators, or have acquired counselling skills to help them in the process.

However, this is all very difficult to reconcile from a professional perspective. For example, Ravizza and Fazio (2002) and others, have claimed that the most important factor in the success of work as a sport psychologist, is not the ability to design a psychological skills intervention, but is based upon your capacity to relate to the other person. If they are correct in this assessment, then the education and training of most aspiring sport psychologists is far from helpful in this regard. Indeed, it could not even be remedied by teaching counselling skills (although this may help a little) because this view is advocating that it is nothing less than the development of personal qualities, our personalities themselves, that is the most important task. The existential psychology approach is in complete agreement here and has of course much to say about what this would mean in practice. Their view, for example, would be similar to that expressed by Corlett (1996) from a different perspective, that sport psychologists should be educated and trained to develop their self-awareness and grow in self-knowledge. May (1967) has argued that the best preparation for this is to encourage self-reflection, and to engage in a thorough and critical study of the key literature contained within the humanities and arts. These writers (consistent with an existential psychology view) insist that psychological work with another person is as much an art as a science, and therefore our training and education should reflect this fact. This has been supported within counselling psychology to a great extent. The widespread use of the scientist-practitioner model to describe the role of the counselling psychologist (Woolfe, 1996), captures some of this issue in stressing that their work must be informed by research, whilst being oriented towards the client as a person.

Another difficulty has been that some sport psychologists have tended for reasons of professional competency to apply strict demarcations between their function and that of counselling psychologists. This has resulted in an attempt to differentiate between educational sport psychologists who are primarily concerned with teaching mental skills and clinically trained sport psychologists. These individuals are qualified to deal with MST based issues or potentially harmful and pathological conditions, such as depression, obsessive behaviour and eating disorders. However, this apparently neat and tidy model is riven with a number of major flaws. The most important of these relates to the frequent failure to distinguish between clinical psychology and counselling. Confusion on this issue is evident in the recent work of Anderson and Clarke (2002) within sport psychology. They appear to view counselling psychology as something that deals with remedial issues such as burn out and eating disorders. This begs the question of what special competency and knowledge do clinical psychologists possess? Indeed, this view is highlighted in the work of Cox *et al.* (1993), and Anderson and Clark (following earlier United States Olympic Committee guidelines), who have identified three categories of sport psychologists: researchers, educators or clinical *and* counselling sport psychologists. However, within the parent discipline of psychology, attention has been devoted to clearly identifying the significant differences between clinical and counselling psychology (e.g. Woolfe and Dryden, 1996). Clinical work evolved in response to the need to treat people with severe mental problems, often within hospital settings. The medical orientation, and training and education of clinicians reflects its focus on the, 'assessment and treatment of persons with significant degrees of psychological disturbance. Words such as clinical and patient are evocative of an illness and treatment orientation' (Woolfe, 1996: 8). In contrast, counselling psychology is primarily about helping people to *function more fully*, to develop their potential and improve their sense of *well being*. In addition, the competing paradigms are equally capable of addressing narrow or less serious issues, or more deep rooted and extensive problems. These may be causing unhappiness or discomfort in a person's life and could also be impacting negatively on their capacity to perform in a particular area. The dominant view in sport psychology is that counselling is about helping athletes with life crises and *not equally* concerned with performance enhancement. This seems to reveal a lack of understanding of the predominantly humanistic psychology base of counselling psychology, where the focus is on helping healthy people achieve their potential (i.e. self-actualization) and to reach optimal performance more often throughout every part of their lives.

A further weakness with many of the opinions expressed on the roles and functions of sport psychologists (e.g. Anderson and Clarke, 2002), is that they fail to consider that broader life issues of a non-clinical nature often interfere with sports performance as much as more specific task related issues. In other words, the reality of work with athletes is that often it is matters like coach relationships, dealing with media, financial concerns, moving clubs and changing roles which are more important. The resolution of these broader life issues only requires input from a clinical sport psychologist where they have been identified or diagnosed as clinical problems. If most sport psychologists are unable to deal with these issues facing the athlete, then the solution is to address the gaps in our education and supervised training, rather than referring the sports performer to a clinician when their problems are not clinical!

Personal reflections

Numerous discussions with other applied sport psychologists have led me to believe that the broader life issues are more often the areas where sports performers seek support from sport psychologists. For example, a full-time sport psychologist working at the highest levels and with serious sports performers has claimed that MST represents no more than 5–10 per cent of his role. Their main work is dealing with contextual and organizational issues and in working with players and performers on broader concerns. They point out that dealing with homesickness, relationship issues, and more profound matters like developing self-awareness and personal growth for example, influence sporting performance more than anything else (personal communication). This is rather ironic because their university education at undergraduate and postgraduate level like many others, has not given them the requisite skills and knowledge for this current role. However, unlike some sport psychologists working at lower levels or in publicly funded programmes, these sport psychologists have been unable to offer MST because of the environmental constraints in such a ruthless performance and results focused milieu. In blunt language, they have had to meet the *needs* of the sports performers rather than being able to force mental skills based programmes upon the athletes, as has been happening all too often in the past and elsewhere.

It seems that many applied sport psychologists are having to deal with a myriad of issues which fall outside of clinical psychology and are not likely to be successfully addressed by MST. Much of what is being done resembles counselling, however, it is often being delivered by sport psychologists with little or no background in this branch of the discipline. Given this, is it any wonder that some see sport psychology as 'just' talking, with the occasional 'flashy' technique like visualization or progressive muscular relaxation thrown in for good measure?

It is against this scenario that existential psychology approaches to counselling in sport psychology can provide an appealing alternative. As has been discussed throughout this book, existential approaches to sport psychology rely much less on the application of techniques and place a far greater emphasis on the personal qualities of the individual psychologist. In particular, it is the qualities of empathy, authenticity and presence that are considered to be essential to the success of an existential encounter. During one-to-one meetings with sports performers, I increasingly became aware that it was by providing an opportunity for dialogue that my most important work could occur. This was clearly experienced during a research study comparing the effectiveness of different anxiety control interventions in competitive ice skating (Nesti and Sewell, 1997). Interview data post-intervention revealed that at least for elite female youth ice skaters, specific MST programmes aimed at anxiety control were much less effective than simply talking with each young performer. The control group involved skaters in a one-to-one discussion of a general nature, with a sport psychologist for 15 minutes each week, over eight weeks. No attempt was made to direct the skaters' attention to anxiety, motivation or any other aspect of their skating experience. The approach used by the sport psychologist followed Rogers' (1961) client-centred therapy, which emphasizes amongst other things, that a non-directive approach be adopted by the therapist or psychologist. Although no effort was directed at developing self-awareness, self-knowledge or psychological skills, there was clear evidence that the skaters were nevertheless stimulated (albeit indirectly) by the sessions to consider their relationship to skating and broader life issues. This was powerfully expressed by one of the skaters from the control group in the following way:

> Sometimes something just clicks and before you know it, and you can't stop it even if you wanted to, you find yourself thinking about the real big stuff and where you fit in. I don't know whether it was caused by these meetings, or maybe it was the right time, but recently I've started looking at things differently, deeper and more real, and laughing at all this stuff, the jealousies, and sick stuff like that, and I've never felt so calm and strong.
>
> (Nesti, 1999)

Another skater in the group revealed that they found the chance to talk confidentially to someone interested in their sport and who treated them as individuals brought very specific benefits. She claimed that:

> These sessions have made me think about myself and where I'm going in skating and whether I am as good as I think I am. I don't really remember what we talked about at each session, but I have started to wonder a bit more about what I really want and to think about the times that I've blown

it. I always talk to my coach about how I'm doing and where I can get to with tests and competitions but I've never really asked myself these questions until these last few weeks!

(Nesti, 1999)

The strength of these views and that I continued to come across similar feedback with other skaters in the control group, seemed to provide further validation for the approach of existential psychology. At a basic level the existential view requires the sport psychologist to engage in an open dialogue with a person who happens to be someone who also takes part in competitive sport. Here is a psychological approach that from its core philosophical foundation is fully oriented towards fulfilling what Martens (1987) demanded of sport psychology that we consider, the person first, and the athlete second! Through use of an existential perspective I was able to understand that when athletes sometimes spoke about helpful nerves and needing to feel anxious before major events to perform optimally, they were often talking about normal anxiety. It will be remembered that according to the existentialists, this anxiety is still often very uncomfortable but is nevertheless an unavoidable accompaniment of facing an important challenge and is frequently beneficial to performance.

The existential counselling framework also allowed me to focus on developing the personal qualities necessary to engage in an intense dialogical encounter with another person. Through reflecting on my applied experience it became easier to understand the existential psychology view that techniques, such as the use of specific listening skills, mirroring and other behaviours, could obscure the deeply personal communication demanded within the existential approach. This emphasis on being authentic at all costs means that the existential approach is available to all. The only requirement is that when one person (a sport psychologist) meets another person (a sports performer) both parties should assess the success of the encounter on the directness and power of the communication. It is not a matter of *style* but a question of *substance*. Applied sport psychologists who are dissatisfied with much of the dominant approach in the discipline are likely to be confused and disappointed to hear that there are very few technical skills or techniques used by existential psychologists to guide their sessions, or to provide for their clients to use. When asked what needs to be done to operate from within an existential paradigm, the answer tends to be rather surprising for some and unwelcome to many. At its most basic level, this approach asks the sport psychologist to be themselves, and in their own unique and individual way to throw themselves into an encounter with another person where the qualities of presence, authenticity and empathy will be experienced in *a dialogue of passion, spontaneity and reflection*. The training towards this requires the sport psychologist to critically reflect on their work with each athlete, to eschew the use of techniques within their sessions and to immerse themselves in the existential literature. The result will be a person educated in greater self-understanding of the fundamentals of good human communication, rather than a ten point step-by-step set of instructions on how to do it!

A constant exposure to existential psychology literature has allowed me to locate my work within a framework that I can use to inform an understanding of what has been discussed with the client. It has provided me with a paradigm that I can draw upon to interpret my case notes, and to assist me when I prepare records and reports. I use this written material to assist the sports performer to gain a deeper and more clarified view of the issues facing them. At times, these written accounts can be used within the encounter, especially at the beginning, to aid the process of dialogue. For example, the sport psychologist and sports performer may set time aside at the start of a session to quietly read this material. This can be helpful in drawing out some of the key existential issues confronting the person, and can be used as a way to establish a connection between the sport psychologist and their client prior to their encounter. Where the work is constrained due to time availability, this may also help the approach to be more directive without restricting the work to focusing on specific goals or set targets. In relation to this, it has pointed out that time-limited existential counselling is possible and in fact can be beneficial because:

> With only twelve or so weeks to work in, however, clients are confronted with the fact that any change will inevitably be limited. The time-limited nature of the therapeutic process, then, encourages clients to reduce their expectations to feasible and workable levels ... and that the constant reminder of the ending will intensify a client's commitment to the therapeutic process, encouraging the client to bring to the fore anxieties or concerns that, in a less time-pressurised environment, she might tend to withhold.
>
> (Cooper, 2003: 131)

Whether long term or more brief and directive, existential approaches can be used by anyone operating in sport psychology. There is no need to learn particular skills or techniques, however, there is a requirement to study, critically discuss and engage fully in the writings of existential philosophy and of those psychologists who have used this perspective in their applied work. Unfortunately, to date this has meant that interested sport psychologists have in the main had to consider literature from existential psychology, given that so few have written about this approach in sport settings. However, this is not the first time that we have had to borrow from the parent discipline of psychology! The history and development of sport psychology is largely one of taking ideas, concepts and theories from established areas in psychology and adapting these where necessary, to reflect the sporting context. In my own situation, I had an opportunity to study existential-phenomenological psychology on a masters degree programme at the University of Alberta and to pursue this further within a PhD in psychology at Hull University. This has given me a very different grounding to many of my sports colleagues. Although very different to most of the psychology that sport psychologists have been exposed to, existential ideas and the aims of existential psychology are easily recognizable to experienced applied sport psychologists. Once it is possible to grasp some of the key terms like authenticity, meaning and its view of anxiety, my view is that, in particular for those working one-to-one with sports performers, much of what existential psychologists have to say will resonate strongly with many in the profession.

Self-knowledge and beyond!

A close examination of existential psychology reveals that this approach is interested in helping people to become more fully themselves. It is argued that through this, we are able to see more clearly who we truly are, and as a consequence be better prepared to choose and take the often difficult decisions in our lives on the journey towards fulfilling our potential. Until quite recently, most of psychology viewed our physical and psychological needs as representing the sum total of what it means to be a human being. However, some writers within existential psychology have argued against this and have included references to the spiritual within their accounts. The most prominent of these individuals is Frankl (1969), who developed his approach throughout his life and most importantly after spending years in a Nazi concentration camp during World War II. The experiences there and later work within his therapeutic practice, convinced him that the individual's main task in life is to find a source of meaning that will provide some form of *ultimate meaning in their lives*. His existential approach has been referred to as logo therapy – *Logos* being Greek for '*meaning*'. Frankl draws on the work of phenomenologists like Max Scheler and existential philosophers such as Marcel (1948). According to the views of Frankl, Scheler and Marcel, an individual is made up of mind, body *and spirit*, and it is the spirit which is the most important and unique aspect of the human person. Indeed, there are even times where in circumstances of physical hardship and psychological deprivation, the survival of the individual rests upon the existence of the spirit. Frankl describes how this became clear to him as he witnessed the power of human spirit in the appalling conditions of physical and psychological brutality within the concentration camps. Frankl's view that there is a need to search for some form of ultimate meaning in our lives has been subject to criticism from Yalom (1980), Cooper (2003) and from within the existentialism of Camus (1955) and Sartre (1958). For these psychologists and thinkers, appeals to some higher or 'super' meaning are ways in which individuals abandon their freedom and choices in their lives. As has been discussed in Chapters 1 and 2, the view of Sartre and others that life has no meaning except the meaning I give it, does not represent a neutral position either.

There are psychologists within the existential tradition (e.g. Valle, 1989) or close to it (e.g. Assagioli, 1993), for whom the re-integration of a consideration of the spiritual dimension has been welcomed. The study of spirituality within psychology has grown in recent years. For example, Shafranske (1996), Seligman and Csikszentmihalyi (2000) and Argyle (2002), have considered the importance of spiritual dimensions in their work. Within sport psychology,

Csikszentmihalyi's (1975, 1990) work on flow and Ravizza's (1977) study of peak experiences have included reference to spiritual elements. There has been a growing interest in the important role that spirituality can play in enhancing sports performance by contributing to personal growth and well being. From a more applied perspective, Ravizza (2002b) has highlighted that the sport psychology consultant should include spirituality and spiritual issues within an athlete-centred model that seeks to enhance sports performance and personal fulfilment. Czech *et al.* (2004) utilized a phenomenological method to analyse interviews from elite athletes and discovered that prayer and/or spiritual rituals are often used in competitive sport. Techniques to assist spiritual development in sports performers include the use of reflective writing, contemplation, listening to music, meditation, creative activities and spending time with family and close friends. Much existential psychology, as has been discussed, recognizes that spirituality and transcendental beliefs are important sources of personal meaning for many, including those performing and participating in sport.

Personal reflections

During the past 17 years' experience of working in applied sport psychology, I have frequently encountered situations where sports performers have had to find the strength to keep moving forwards in moments of great physical and psychological difficulty. These periods were often filled with doubt and anxiety, and usually took place at what Yalom (1999) has called, boundary situations. For example, at an individual level, this may be when facing a major sports injury, significant change in personal circumstances or shift in responsibilities. Within team settings, examples could include the threat of relegation, the introduction of new practices and major tactical alternations and changes in team managers or coaches. At these moments, and during others where great demands are placed upon the sports performer (e.g. prior to a crucial match or event), it was not uncommon for individuals to start looking for something beyond their strictly physical and psychological needs. This took many forms. For some, it could lead to discussion and reflection on the frequently used term in competitive sport, *team spirit*. For others such as coaches, they would ask how the sport psychologist could help them develop more spirited performances from their athletes. Players and coaching staff would frequently refer to other teams, groups or individuals as being, 'full of spirit' or possessing, 'real spirit'. My reflections on the frequent use of this language, especially at 'crisis' moments, led me to clarify that at least within some traditions of existential psychology, the concept of spirit had been considered seriously. The response of some others in sport psychology who I have worked with, has been to either dismiss the term as being religious and therefore outside of their legitimate concerns, or to translate spirit to mean self-belief or self-confidence. However, my experiences with sports performers convinced me that they were not talking about self-confidence, and in most cases, neither did they expect a religious account of spirit. Instead, they assumed that psychology and especially sport psychology would have something to offer on team spirit and spirited performances, which after all, are some of the most frequently used terms in competitive sport!

During existential encounters with several sports performers, there were also occasions where the work was oriented towards the search for meaning and any discussions around spirit emerged slowly, rather than being an initial and explicit concern. Where an athlete and a sport psychologist have worked together over a significant period, as in the example case study shown below, and build a close and trusting relationship, the potential for broader life issues and existential concerns including spiritual factors to emerge in counselling is far greater.

Case study

The following relates to work done with a UK-based international level competitive athlete, during the preparatory phase before participation in the world championships. The sport psychologist and the athlete had been working together over a period of two years; this involved 17 one-to-one meetings or encounters (as existential psychology would describe them) unevenly spread across this time. The material considered here emerged from the final two meetings with the sport psychologist before the sports performer left to join their team at a pre-championship's overseas training camp.

The athlete discussed that although they had been training well and receiving positive feedback from the coaches, sports scientists and others working with them, there were still matters that in their view required attention. The athlete attempted to articulate what this 'gap' referred to and began to describe that they did not feel as fully prepared as on other recent occasions during the final phases before a major competitive event. With the guidance of the sport psychologist, the athlete began a closer examination of what this missing element felt like, how it was experienced in their sporting and broader life (if at all), and whether it was something that they had encountered before. The athlete provided a rich account of this factor that initially they labelled as, 'X'. After a patient and careful scrutiny of factor X had been achieved between the sport psychologist and the athlete, it became increasingly clear that this element did not fit neatly into the more familiar terms of applied academic sport psychology, such as confidence, self-esteem or motivation. The sports person emphasized that this factor X felt like 'the centre that holds the whole thing together' and at another time, as a 'kind of mysterious bit that I know only when it is not there! ... And that when it is not with me or distant and weak I feel incomplete even if at one level everything looks like it is going really well'. During these two encounters the athlete was encouraged to consider how they might be able to begin to address this need. Initially this proved to be a very difficult task because of the desire to think about this factor X as something which could be approached in a similar fashion to other elements of performance preparation, like MST, strength training or technical improvements. It became increasingly clear to the athlete that they were quite familiar with what they needed to do to allow for the growth of factor X, having managed this at several other international and top domestic competitive events throughout their career. Although still reticent to consider *that x most likely referred to 'the spirit'*, the athlete was able to clarify how they had vivid experience of the reality of this factor before the last Olympics, and that they had done a number of things which made them feel a very powerful mixture of calm serenity, deep self-confidence and prepared to place their whole *self* on the line as though their life literally depended on it. The athlete began to recognize that paradoxically, to feed this meant that they had to broaden their focus to issues outside of immediate performance concerns and training, and sometimes do less and with less intensity, and in their own words to be 'unprofessional in order to be more professional'. This final observation relates to the need to accept that without leaving or making space for factor X, it cannot be accommodated; this space must be created and protected by the athlete even at the expense of dropping other important responsibilities and agreed tasks. The sport psychologist assisted the athlete in this by suggesting that they listen to music, walk in the hills, visit friends and close relations, read literary classics and devote time to self-reflection and contemplation. These and other activities were engaged in by the athlete during this period and they began to feel that they were beginning, in their own words, 'to fill the void' which they had been increasingly aware of as the competition got nearer. Towards the end of the second meeting the athlete began to use the terms 'spirit' and 'factor X' interchangeably when describing this work that they were doing and its effects. It became quite clear that a major obstacle to expressing this in terms of spirit and spiritual development was that the sports performer felt uncomfortable with language most usually associated with religion and theology, and that this facet of their life was not something that you could expect to discuss with a sport psychologist. Once the athlete accepted that what they were experiencing could be discussed within a broader framework of psychology (i.e. existential psychology), it became possible for there to be a deeper engagement around how spiritual development could enhance sports performance. The athlete expressed a strong interest in reading literature dealing with this factor in sport to better understand their own experience and needs in this area of their lives, and to be more aware of practical ways of increasing spiritual strength for sports performance. Unfortunately, literature in applied sport psychology that specifically deals with the importance of the spirit and spiritual growth and how athletes (and others) can assist this process is largely missing from the field. This was partly remedied by guiding the athlete towards a disparate collection of material from philosophy, theology, mainstream psychology and other disciplines where some consideration has been given to these questions. Whilst helpful in many ways these books and articles are not always easy to digest or connect to the experience of high-level competitive sport. In addition to reading more broadly, the sports performer began to strengthen their ties with close family members whilst at the same time significantly reducing their contact with the media, agents, business acquaintances and others. This withdrawing from their normal world, which they characterized as often involving a large amount of ceaseless and unproductive activity and a renewed effort at deepening the most personally important relationships, was viewed by the athlete as part of their spiritual re-awakening. This strategy and others aimed at developing the spirit, made them feel even more prepared, and stronger mentally and spiritually for the major challenge ahead.

At the highest level of sport there are testimonies beginning to emerge in relation to this aspect of performance and personal development. For example, Olympic triple jump champion Jonathon Edwards claimed that just after the 1996 Atlanta Olympics, he experienced a crisis of meaning in his life and his jumping had become negatively affected by this. It was through reading a book on personal meaning by the existential psychologist Victor Frankl (1984), that Edwards found spiritual guidance and direction, and he began to regain a sense of joy in what he was doing.

These and other similar accounts support the use of an existential psychology approach in applied work. Existential psychology recognizes that spirituality, and spiritual and transcendental beliefs, are important sources of personal meaning for many, including those involved in sport. Hopefully, this view will encourage future researchers and sport psychology practitioners to accommodate these important terms within their work.

References

Alpert, R. and Haber, R.N. (1960) 'Anxiety in academic achievement situations', *Journal of Abnormal and Social Psychology*, 61: 207–215.

Andersen, M.B. (ed.) (2000) *Doing Sport Psychology*, Champaign, IL: Human Kinetics.

Anderson, A. and Clarke, P. (2002) 'Afterword', in D. Lavallee and I. Cockerill (eds), *Counselling in Sport and Exercise Contexts*, Leicester: British Psychological Society, pp. 69–73.

Anderson, A.G., Miles, A., Mahoney, C. and Robinson, P. (2002) 'Evaluating the effectiveness of applied sport psychology practice: making the case for a case study approach', *The Sport Psychologist*, 16: 432–453.

Argyle, M. (2002) *Psychology and Religion: An Introduction*, London: Routledge.

Assagioli, R. (1993) *Psychosynthesis: A Manual of Principles and Techniques*, London: Harper Collins Publishers.

Balague, G. (1999) 'Understanding identity, value and meaning when working with elite athletes', *The Sport Psychologist*, 13: 89–98.

Bassett-Short, A. and Hammel, G.A. (1995) 'Existential psychology from within the training process', in K.J. Schneider and R. May (eds), *The Psychology of Existence*, New York: McGraw-Hill, pp. 125–131.

Berdyaev, N.A. (1937) *The Destiny of Man*, London: Duddington.

Beswick, B. (2000) *Focus for Soccer: Developing a Winning Mental Approach*, Champaign, IL: Human Kinetics.

Bretherton, R. and Ørner, R. (2003) 'Positive psychology in disguise', *The Psychologist*, March, pp. 136–137.

Buber, M. (1958) *I and Thou*; trans. R.G. Smith, Edinburgh: T. and T. Clark, New York: Charles Scribner's Sons.

Buber, M. (1970) *I and Thou*; trans. W. Kaufmann, New York: Charles Scribner's Sons.

Bull, S. and Shambrook, C. (1998) 'Adherence to mental skills training and issues of service delivery', *Journal of Sport Sciences*, 16: 75–88.

Butler, R.J. (1997) *Sport Psychology in Performance*, Oxford: Butterworth-Heinemann.

Calhoun, L.G. and Tedeschi, R.G. (1998) 'Posttraumatic growth: future directions', in R.G. Tedeschi, C.L. Park and L.G. Calhoun (eds), *Posttraumatic Growth*, Mahwah, NJ: Lawrence Erlbaum, pp. 215–238.

Camus, A. (1955) *The Myth of Sisyphus*; trans. J. O'Brien, London: Penguin (Original work published 1942).

Cannon, B. (1991) *Sartre and Psychoanalysis: An Existential Challenge to Clinical Meta-theory*, Lawrence, KS: University Press of Kansas.

Caruso, I.A. (1964) *Existential Psychology: From Analysis to Synthesis*, London: Darton, Longman & Todd.

Chesterton, G.K. (1910/1994) *What's Wrong With the World*, San Francisco, CA: Ignatius Press.

Clark, L.A. and Watson, D. (1988) 'Mood and the mundane: relations between daily life events and self-reported mood', *Journal of Personality and Social Psychology*, 54: 296–308.

Clark, M.T. (1973) *The Problem of Freedom*, New York: Meredith Corporation.

Clough, P., Hockey, R. and Sewell, D. (1996) 'The use of a diary methodology to assess the impact of exercise on mental states', in G. Robson, B. Cripps and H. Steinberg (eds), *Qualitative and Quantitative Research Methods in Sport and Exercise Psychology*, Leicester, England: British Psychological Society, pp. 22–27.

Cockerill, I. (ed.) (2002) *Solutions in Sport Psychology*, London: Thomson.

Cohn, H.W. (1997) *Existential Thought and Therapeutic Practice: An Introduction to Existential Psychotherapy*, London: Sage.

Colaizzi, P.F. (1978) 'Psychological research as the phenomenologist views it', in R.S. Valle and M.I. King (eds), *Existential-Phenomenological Alternatives for Psychology*, New York: Oxford University Press.

Cooper, M. (2003) *Existential Therapies*, London: Sage.

Corlett, J. (1996) 'Sophistry, Socrates and sport psychology', *The Sport Psychologist*, 10: 84–94.

Cox, R.H., Qiu, Y. and Liu, Z. (1993) 'Overview of sport psychology', in R.N. Singer, M. Murphy and L.K. Tennat (eds), *Handbook of Research in Sport Psychology*, New York: Macmillan, pp. 3–31.

Csikszentmihalyi, M. (1975) *Beyond Boredom and Anxiety*, San Francisco, CA: Jossey-Bass.

Csikszentmihalyi, M. (1990) *Flow: The Psychology of Optimal Experience*, New York: Harper & Row.

Csikszentmihalyi, M. (1992) *Flow: The Psychology of Happiness*, London: Rider Publications.

Csikszentmihalyi, M. and Csikszentmihalyi, I.S. (1988) *Optimal Experience: Psychological Studies in Flow Consciousness*, Cambridge: Cambridge University Press.

Czech, D.R., Wrisberg, C., Fisher, L., Thompson, C. and Hayes, G. (2004) 'The experience of christian prayer in sport – An Existential Phenomenological Investigation', *Journal of Psychology and Christianity*, 2: 1–19.

Dale, G. (1996) 'Existential-phenomenology: emphasizing the experience of the athlete in sport psychology research', *The Sport Psychologist*, 10: 158–171.

Dale, G. (2000) 'Distractions and coping strategies of elite decathletes during their most memorable performance', *The Sport Psychologist*, 14: 17–41.

Davidson, R.J. and Schwartz, G.E. (1976) 'The psychobiology of relaxation and related states: a multi process theory', in D.I. Mostofky (ed.), *Behavioral Control and Modification of Physiological Activity*, Englewood Cliffs, NJ: Prentice Hall, pp. 399–442.

deCarvalho, R.J. (1996) 'Rollo R. May, (1909–1994): a biographical sketch', *Journal of Humanistic Psychology*, 36: 8–16.

Denny, J.P. (1966) 'The effects of anxiety and intelligence concept formation', *Journal of Experimental Psychology*, 72: 596–602.

Edwards, T. and Hardy, L. (1996) 'The interactive effects of intensity and direction of cognitive and somatic anxiety and self-confidence upon performance', *Journal of Sport and Exercise Psychology*, 18: 296–312.

Fahlberg, L.L., Fahlberg, L.A. and Gates, K.W. (1992) 'Exercise and existence: exercise behaviour from an existential-phenomenological perspective', *The Sport Psychologist*, 6: 172–191.

Fenz, W.D. and Epstein, S. (1967) 'Gradients of physiological arousal in parachutists as a function of an approaching jump', *Psychosomatic Medicine*, 29: 33–51.

Fischer, W. (1970) *Theories of Anxiety*, New York: Harper & Row.

Frankl, V. (1969) *The Will to Meaning: Foundations and Applications of Logotherapy*, New York: Meridan.

Frankl, V. (1984) *Man's Search for Meaning: An Introduction to Logotherapy*, New York: Simon & Schuster.

Freud, S. (1991) *Civilization and its Discontents*, New York: W.W. Norton & Company.

Friedman, M.S. (2002) 'Martin Buber and dialogical psychotherapy', *Journal of Humanistic Psychology*, 42: 7–36.

Fromm, E. (1942) *The Fear of Freedom*, London: Ark Paperbacks.

Fromm, E. (1994) *The Art of Listening*, London: Constable.

Gallwey, T. (1974) *The Inner Game of Tennis*, London: Pan Books.

Gallwey, T. (1979) *The Inner Game of Golf*, USA: Random House.

Geller, L. (1982) 'The failure of Self-Actualization Theory: a critique of Carl Rogers and Abraham Maslow', *Journal of Humanistic Psychology*, 22: 56–73.

Gill, D.L. (1994) 'A sport and exercise perspective on stress', *Quest*, 46: 20–27.

Giorgi, A. (1970) *Psychology as a human science*, New York: Harper & Row.

Giorgi, A. (1985) *Phenomenology and Psychological Research*, Pittsburgh, PA: Duquesne University Press.

Goldenberg, H. and Isaacson, Z. (1996) 'Between persons: the narrow ridge where I and thou meet', *Journal of the Society for Existential Analysis*, 7: 118–130.

Gordon, A. (1990) 'A mental skills training program for the Western Australia State Cricket Team', *The Sport Psychologist*, 4: 386–399.

Gould, D., Finch, L.M. and Jackson, S. (1993) 'Coping strategies used by National Champion Figure Skaters', *The Sport Psychologist*, 64: 453–468.

Greenspan, M.J. and Feltz, D. (1989) 'Psychological interventions with athletes in competitive situations: a review', *The Sport Psychologist*, 4: 369–377.

Hall, H.K., Kerr, A.W. and Matthews, J. (1998) 'Precompetitive anxiety in sport: the contribution of achievement goals and perfectionism', *The Sport Psychologist*,

Hanin, Y. and Syrja, R. (1995) 'Performance affect in junior ice hockey players: an application of the individual zone of optimal functioning model', *The Sport Psychologist*, 9: 169–187.

Hartley, S. (1999) *MST or Socratic Sport Psychology*, unpublished Masters Thesis, Leeds Metropolitan University.

Heidegger, M. (1962) *Being and Time*, New York: Harper & Row.

Hergenhahn, B.R. (1999) *An Introduction to Theories of Personality*, Hamline University: Prentice-Hall.

Hill, K.L. (2001) *Frameworks for Sport Psychologists: Enhancing Sport Performance*, Champaign, IL: Human Kinetics.

Husserl, E. (1970) *The Crisis of European Sciences and Transcendental Phenomenology*; trans. D. Carr, Evanston, IL: Northwestern University Press.

Ihde, D. (1986) *Experimental Phenomenology: An Introduction*, Albany, NY: State University of New York Press.

Jackson, S.A. and Csikszentmihalyi, M. (1999) *Flow in Sports: The Key to Optimal Experiences and Performances*, Champaign, IL: Human Kinetics.

Johnson, M.S. and Butryn, T.M. (2002) 'The sport phenomenon: an experiential guide to phenomenological research and interviewing in sport', Proceedings of the Annual Conference of the American Association of Applied Sports Psychology: Tucson, Arizona, 30 October–3 November 2002.

Jones, G. (1995) 'More than just a game: research developments and issues in competitive anxiety in sport', *British Journal of Psychology*, 86: 449–478.

Jones, G., Hanton, S. and Swain, A.B.J. (1994) 'Intensity and interpretation of anxiety symptoms in elite and non-elite sports performers', *Personality and Individual Differences*, 17: 657–663.

Jones, G. and Hardy, L. (1990) *Stress and Performance in Sport*, Chichester, England: Wiley.

Jones, G., Swain, A. and Harwood, C. (1996) 'Positive and negative affect as predictors of competitive anxiety', *Personality and Individual Differences*, 20: 107–114.

Jones, M., Mace, R. and Stockbridge, C. (1997) 'The importance of measuring athletes' emotional states during sports performance', in I. Cockerill and H. Steinberg (eds), *Cognitive Enhancement in Sport and Exercise Psychology*, Leicester: British Psychological Society, Sport and Exercise Psychology Section, pp. 44–49.

Kerr, J.H. (1997) *Motivation and Emotion in Sport: Reversal Theory*, Hove, England: Psychology Press Ltd.

Kerr, J.H. (2001) *Counselling Athletes: Applying Reversal Theory*, London: Routledge.

Kerry, D.S. and Armour, K.M. (2000) 'Sport sciences and the promise of phenomenology: philosophy, method and insight', *Quest*, 52: 1–17.

Kierkegaard, S. (1844/1944) *The Concept of Dread*; trans. S. Lowrie, Princeton, NJ: Princeton University Press (Originally published in Danish, 1844).

Kingston, F. (1961) *French Existentialism: A Christian Critique*, London: Oxford University Press.

Lane, A. and Terry, P. (1998) 'Mood states as predictors of performance: a conceptual model', *Journal of Sports Sciences*, 16: 93–94.

Lane, A.M., Sewell, D.F., Terry, P.C., Bartram, D. and Nesti, M.S. (1999) 'Confirmatory factor analysis of the competitive state anxiety inventory', *Journal of Sport Sciences*, 17 (6): 505–512.

Lavallee, D. and Cockerill, I. (eds) (2002) *Counselling in Sport and Exercise Contexts*, Leicester: The British Psychological Society, Sport and Exercise Psychology Section.

Lavallee, D., Nesti, M., Borkoles, E., Cockerill, I. and Edge, A. (2000) 'Intervention strategies for athletes in transition', in D. Lavallee and P. Wylleman (eds), *Career Transitions in Sport: International Perspectives*, Morgantown, WV: Fitness Information Technology, pp. 111–130.

Lazarus, R.S. (2000) 'How emotions influence performance in competitive sports', *The Sport Psychologist*, 14: 229–252.

Lines, D. (2002) 'Counselling within a new spiritual paradigm', *Journal of Humanistic Psychology*, 42: 102–123.

Loehr, J.E. (1991) *The Mental Game*, New York: Plume.

McCleod, J. (1996) 'The humanistic paradigm', in R. Woofe and W. Dryden (eds), *Handbook of Counselling Psychology* (pp. 133–155), London: Sage.

McNair, D.M., Lorr, M. and Droppleman, L.F. (1971) *Manual for the Profile of Mood States*, San Diego, CA: Educational and Industrial Testing Service.

Males, J.R. and Kerr, J.H. (1996) 'Stress, emotion and performance in elite slalom canoeists', *The Sport Psychologist*, 10: 17–36.

Marcel, G. (1948) *The Philosophy of Existence*, London: Harvill.

Martens, R. (1977) *Sport Competition Anxiety Test*, Champaign, IL: Human Kinetics.

Martens, R. (1979) 'About Smocks and Jocks', *Journal of Sport Psychology*, 1: 94–99.

Martens, R. (1987) 'Science, knowledge, and sport psychology', *The Sport Psychologist*, 1: 29–55.

Martens, R., Burton, D., Vealey, R.S., Bump, L.A. and Smith, D.E. (1990) 'The Competitive State Anxiety Inventory – 2', in R. Martens, R. Vealey and D. Burton (eds), *Competitive Anxiety in Sport*, Champaign, IL: Human Kinetics.

Maslow, A.H. (1954) *Motivation and Personality*, New York: Harper & Row.

Maslow, A.H. (1968) *Toward a Psychology of Being*, New York: Van Nostrand Reinhold Company.

May, R. (1967) *Psychology and the Human Dilemma*, New York: Van Nostrand Company.

May, R. (1975) *The Courage to Create*, New York: Norton.

May, R. (1977) *The Meaning of Anxiety*, New York: Ronald Press.

Maynard, I.W. and Cotton, P.C. (1993) 'An investigation of two stress-management techniques in a field setting', *The Sport Psychologist*, 7: 375–387.

Merleau-Ponty, M. (1962) *The Phenomenology of Perception*, London: Routledge.

Ming, S. and Martin, G.L. (1996) 'Single-subject evaluation of a self-talk package for improving figure skating performance', *The Sport Psychologist*, 10: 227–238.

Molnar, D.J. (2002) 'An existential-phenomenological investigation of a division 1 athlete going through a coaching transition', Proceedings of the Annual Conference of the American Association of Applied Sports Psychology: Tucson, Arizona. 30 October–3 November 2002.

Moss, D. (1989) 'Psychotherapy and human experience', in S. Valle, M. King and S. Halling (eds), *Existential-Phenomenological Perspectives in Psychology*, New York: Plenum Press, pp. 193–213.

Neiss, R. (1988) 'Reconceptualising arousal: psychobiological states in motor performance', *Psychological Bulletin*, 103: 345–366.

Nesti, M. (1999) *Anxiety and Sport: Time to Ask What Rather than Why*, Unpublished doctoral dissertation, University of Hull, England.

Nesti, M. (2001) 'Working in Sports Development', in K. Hylton, P. Bramham, D. Jackson and M. Nesti (eds), *Sports Development: Policy, Process and Practice*, London: Routledge, pp. 195–213.

Nesti, M. (2002) 'Meaning not measurement: existential psychology approaches to counselling in sport contexts', in D. Lavallee and I. Cockerill (eds), *Counselling in Sport and Exercise Contexts*, Leicester: British Psychological Society, Sport and Exercise Psychology Section, pp. 38–47.

Nesti, M. (2004) 'McDonalds or a Mediterranean feast', Paper Presented at 1st International Conference in Qualitative Research in Sport and Exercise, Liverpool, England.

Nesti, M.S. and Sewell, D. (1997) 'Anxiety control and performance in figure skating', in I. Cockerill and H. Steinberg (eds), *Cognitive Enhancement in Sport and Exercise Psychology*, Leicester: The British Psychological Society.

Nesti, M. and Sewell, D. (1999) 'Losing it: the importance of anxiety and mood stability in sport', *Journal of Personal and Interpersonal Loss*, 4: 257–268.

Orlick, T. (2000) *In Pursuit of Excellence: How to Win in Sport and Life Through Mental Training*, Champaign, IL: Human Kinetics.

Oxendine, J.B. (1970) 'Emotional arousal and motor performance', *Quest*, 13: 23–32.

Parkinson, B., Totterdell, P., Briner, R. and Reynolds, S. (1996) *Changing moods: The Psychology of Mood and Regulation*, New York: Longman Ltd.

Petitpas, A.J., Brewer, B.W. and Van Raalte, J.L. (1996) 'Transitions of the student-athlete: theoretical, empirical, and practical perspectives', in E.F. Etzel, A.P. Ferrante and J.W. Pinckney (eds), *Counselling College Student-Athletes: Issues and Interventions*, 2nd edn, Morgantown, WV: Fitness Information Technology, pp. 137–156.

Pieper, J. (1989) *Josef Pieper: An Anthology*, San Francisco, CA: Ignatius Press.

Polkinghorne, D.E. (1989) 'Phenomenological research methods', in R.S. Valle and S. Halling (eds), *Existential-Phenomenological Perspectives in Psychology*, New York: Plenum Press, pp. 41–60.

Raffety, B.D., Smith, R.E. and Tacek, P. (1997) 'Facilitating and debilitating trait anxiety, situational anxiety, and coping with an anticipated stressor: a process analysis', *Journal of Personality and Social Psychology*, 72: 892–906.

Ravizza, K. (1977) 'Peak experiences in sport', *Journal of Humanistic Psychology*, 17: 35–40.

Ravizza, K. (2002a) 'A philosophical construct: a framework for performance enhancement', *International Journal of Sport Psychology*, 33: 4–18.

Ravizza, K. (2002b) 'Spirituality and peak experiences', Symposia Conducted at the Annual Conference of the American Association of Applied Sports Psychology, Tucson, Arizona.

Ravizza, K. and Fazio, J. (2002) 'Consulting with confidence: using who you are to evoke excellence in others', Workshop Conducted at the Annual Conference of the American Association of Applied Sports Psychology, Tucson, Arizona.

Rennie, D. (1994) 'Human science in counselling psychology: closing the gap between research and practice', Paper Presented at Annual Conference of BPS Division of Counselling Psychology.

Roberts, D.E. (1957) *Existentialism and Religious Belief*, New York: Oxford University Press.

Rogers, C.R. (1961) *On Becoming a Person: A Therapist's View of Psychotherapy*, Boston, MA: Houghton Mifflin.

Rotella, R. (1990) 'Providing sport psychology consulting services to professional athletes', *The Sport Psychologist*, 4: 409–417.

Russell, W.D. and Cox, R.H. (2000) 'A laboratory investigation of positive and negative affect within individual zones of optimal functioning theory', *Journal of Sport Behaviour*, 23: 164–180.

Salter, D. (1997) 'Measure, analyse and stagnate: towards a radical psychology of sport', in R.J. Butler (ed.), *Sports Psychology in Performance*, Oxford: Reed Educational and Professional Publishing Ltd, pp. 248–260.

Sartre, J.P. (1958) *Being and Nothingness: An Essay on Phenomenological Ontology*; trans. H. Barnes, London: Routledge (Original work published 1943).

Schimmack, U. and Diener, H. (1997) 'Affect intensity: separating intensity and frequency in repeatedly measured effect', *Journal of Personality and Social Psychology*, 73: 1313–1329.

Schneider, K.J. (1995) 'Therapeutic applications of existential–integrative psychology', in K.J. Schneider and R. May (eds), *The Psychology of Existence*, New York: McGraw-Hill, pp. 135–183.

Schneider, K.J. and May, R. (eds) (1995) *The Psychology of Existence: An Integrative Clinical Perspective*, New York: McGraw-Hill.

Seligman, M.E.P. and Csikszentmihalyi, M. (2000) 'Positive psychology: an introduction', *American Psychologist*, 55: 5–14.

Selye, H. (1956) *The Stress of Life*, New York: McGraw-Hill.

Sewell, D.F., Clough, P.J. and Robertshaw, L. (1996) 'Exercise addiction, mood and body image, a complex interrelationship', in J. Annett, B. Cripps and H. Steinberg (eds), *Exercise Addiction Motivation for Participation in Sport and Exercise*, Leicester: The British Psychological Society, Sport and Exercise Psychology Section.

Shafranske, E.P. (ed.) (1996) *Religion and the Clinical Practice of Psychology*, Washington, DC: American Psychological Association.

Skinner, B.F. (1974) *About Behaviourism*, New York: Vintage.

Sparkes, A. (2002) *Telling Tales in Sport and Physical Activity: A Qualitative Journey*, Champaign, IL: Human Kinetics Press.

Spielberger, C.D. (1966) *Anxiety and Behaviour*, New York: Academic Press.

Spinelli, E. (1989) *The Interpreted World*, London: Sage.

Spinelli, E. (1994) *Demystifying Therapy*, London: Constable.

Spinelli, E. (1996) 'The existential-phenomenological paradigm', in R. Woolfe and W. Dryden (eds), *Handbook of Counselling Psychology*, London: Sage Publications, pp. 180–200.

Stone, A.A., Neal, J.M. and Shiffman, S. (1993) 'Daily assessments of stress and coping and their association with mood', *Annals of Behavioural Medicine*, 15: 8–16.

Swain, A. and Jones, G. (1992) 'Relationships between sport achievement orientation and competitive state anxiety', *The Sport Psychologist*, 6: 42–54.

Terry, P.C. (1995) 'Discriminant capability of performance mood state profiling amongst athletes: a review and synthesis', *The Sport Psychologist*, 9: 245–260.

Valle, R.S. (1989) 'The emergence of transpersonal psychology', in R.S. Valle, M. King and S. Halling (eds), *Existential-Phenomenological Perspectives in Psychology*, London: Plenum Press, pp. 3–16.

Valle, R.S., King, M. and Halling, S. (1989) *Existential-Phenomenological Perspectives in Psychology*, London: Plenum Press.

Van Deurzen-Smith, E. (1988) *Existential Counselling in Practice*, London: Sage.

Van Deurzen-Smith, E. (2002) *Existential Counselling and Psychotherapy in Practice*, 2nd edn, London: Sage.

Van Kaam, A. (1969) *Existential Foundations of Psychology*, New York: Image.

Verbugge, L. (1980) 'Health diaries', *Medical Care*, 18: 73–95.

Von Gebsattel, V.E. (1954) *Prolegama to a Medical Anthropology*, Berlin: Springer Verlag.

Watson, J. (1924) *Behaviourism*, New York: Norton.

Watson, D. and Tellegen, A. (1985) 'Towards a consensual structure of mood', *Psychological Bulletin*, 98: 219–235.

Welsh-Simpson, D. (1998) 'Helping people with existential crises', *Journal of the Society of Existential Analysis*, 9: 17–30.

White, R.W. (1959) 'Motivation reconsidered: the concept of competence', *Psychological Review*, 66: 297–333.

Wilson, P. and Eklund, C. (1998) 'The relationship between competitive anxiety and self-presentational concerns', *The Sports Psychologist*, 13: 178–186.

Woolfe, R. (1996) 'The nature of counselling psychology', in R. Woolfe and W. Dryden (eds), *Handbook of Counselling Psychology*, London: Sage, pp. 3–22.

Woolfe, R. and Dryden, W. (eds) (1996) *Handbook of Counselling Psychology*, London: Sage.

Yalom, I. (1980) *Existential Psychotherapy*, New York: Basic Books.

Yalom, I. (1999) *Momma and the Meaning of Life: Tales of Psychotherapy*, London, Piatkus.

Index

29–32; roots 20; and the sports
performer 35–7; therapy 31; *vs.*
humanistic psychology viii–ix, 3, 9–10,
13–14, 15–16, 73; *see also* existential
counselling
existential psychotherapy *see* existential
counselling
existentialism: ambiguity 27; co-
constitutionality 12, 24; embodied
freedom 26; essence 25; existence 25;
facts 27, 93; goals 28; human being
24–5, 26; human nature 16, 17, 24, 25,
29, 30; mortality 26, 32, 33, 115;
ontological characteristics 28;
philosophical roots 15, 22–7; and
psychology 27–9; self-consciousness 26,
28; situated freedom 12, 14, 24; spiritual
dimension 17, 19, 26, 123–5; truth 12,
27; *see also* freedom
experience 47, 55

facts 27, 93
Fahlberg, L.L. 49, 53–4, 56
fate 28, 76, 94
Fazio, J. 81–2, 117
fear 54, 55, 61
Fenz, W.D. 64
Finch, L.M. 45, 54
Fischer, W. 20, 51, 57, 59, 60, 64
Flow theory 56
football: sport psychologist case study
101–9
Frankl, V. 99, 102, 105, 115, 116, 123, 127
free will 8, 9, 16, 17
freedom 10–12, 20, 27, 28, 29, 30, 32, 34,
115; embodied freedom 26; situated
freedom 12, 14, 24; *see also* choice
Freud, S. 8, 19, 23, 30, 51, 57
Friedman, M.S. 16–17, 19
Fromm, E. 10–11, 51, 75, 83, 84

Gallwey, T. 6
Gates, K.W. 49, 53–4, 56
Geller, L. 13, 14, 19
genuine learning 93–4, 114
Gill, D.L. 53, 61
Giorgi, A. ix, 9, 10, 19, 20, 29–30, 31, 39,
44, 47, 49, 56, 100
global learning 95
God 25, 27, 29
Goldenberg, H. 16, 80
good and evil 14, 28
Gordon, A. 67
Gould, D. 45, 54

guilt 14, 28, 85, 109

Haber, R.N. 65
Hall, H.K. 65
Halling, S. 23, 30, 55–6
Hammel, G.A. 96, 105
Hanin, Y. 53
Hanton, S. 52
Hardy, L. 52, 54, 61, 111
Hartley, S. 7
Harwood, C. 61, 65
Heidegger, M. 25, 29, 40, 108
Hergenhahn, B.R. 33
Hill, K.L. 5, 117
Hockey, R. 65
hope 14
human nature 16, 17, 24, 25, 29, 30
human science ix, 9, 19, 30, 39, 56, 61,
100
Humanism 8, 9, 10–11, 76, 117
humanistic psychology 7–9; counselling 9,
17, 78, 117; existential benefits 16–17;
freedom 11–12; *vs.* existential
psychology viii–ix, 3, 9–10, 13–14,
15–16, 73
Husserl, E. 21, 39, 41, 46
hypnosis 62

ice skating 7, 56, 120
Idealism 22
Ihde, D. 44
I–it mode 31, 81
inauthenticity 76, 84–5
individualized zone of optimal functioning
(IZOF) 53
information acquisition 93
intentionality ix, 28, 39, 45–6
interactionist approach 21
interviews 30, 42–3, 47, 48, 86–7, 92–3,
124
Isaacson, Z. 16, 80
isolation 115
I–Thou relationship 15, 31–2, 43, 81, 82,
83, 113
IZOF (individualized zone of optimal
functioning) 53

Jackson, S. 45, 54
Jackson, S.A. 56
James, W. 41, 46
Jaspers, K. 29
JFK University 117
Johnson, M.S. 49
Jones, G. 52, 53, 54, 59, 61, 63, 65, 111